The Jail:
Mission Field for Churches

THE JAIL

Mission Field
for Churches
━TOM ADAMS━

BROADMAN PRESS
Nashville, Tennessee

Dewey Decimal Classification: 259.5
Subject Heading: CHURCH WORK WITH CRIMINALS
Library of Congress Catalog Number: 85-5928

Printed in the United States of America

Unless otherwise stated, all Scripture quotations are from the King James Version of the Bible.

Scripture quotations marked NIV are from HOLY BIBLE, *New International Version*, copyright © 1978, New York Bible Society. Used by permission.

Library of Congress Cataloging in Publication Data

Adams, Tom, 1924-
    The jail : mission field for churches.

    Bibliography: p.
    1. Church work with prisoners.   2. Chaplains,
Prison.   I. Title.
BV4340.A33   1985   259'.5   85-5928
ISBN 0-8054-2002-9 (soft)

To my wife Alyce,
whose words "Quit talking and do it"
moved me to complete this book.

Contents

Introduction

Mrs. Willis (not her real name) shared her concern for her grandson with her pastor. Her daughter had told her that he was running around with the wrong crowd and that she was afraid he was into drugs. Sure enough, it was not too long before his name appeared in the newspaper: he had been apprehended during a burglary. The habit he had was requiring more and more money to support, and had finally landed him in the clutches of the law.

The pastor decided to go down to the jail to see the grandson. It was his first time to go to the local lockup for a visit, the only other time being for a worship service on an early Sunday morning conducted by the Gideons. In fact, in twenty-five years as a pastor and home missionary, he had not been inside a correction center of any kind to visit more than half-a-dozen times.

He had a little trouble getting in! The staff members at the "intake" desk did not recognize him and were suspicious of him, even though he produced his business card identifying him as a local minister. After some discussion, they let him in. He had to empty his pockets and be subjected to a search. Then he had a long wait until a guard finally appeared with George (not his real name, either), whom he had met only briefly once before.

Both of them felt ill at ease, he because of the unfamiliarity of his surroundings, and George because a minister was seeing him in this bad light. For once, a preacher fumbled around for some words—what *do* you say in a situation like this? He offered George a New Testament and some tracts, and told him that he would pray for him and be glad to come back to see him if he wanted him to. Though nervous, George seemed glad that someone had come to see him, and asked the pastor to come back.

In a couple of weeks, the pastor did return to the jail for another visit. It was much the same hassle getting in, but the visit went a little more smoothly than the first time. George asked about his grandmother, and seemed ashamed that he had embarrassed her and his family by what he had done. The preacher asked George if he had read any of the New Testament, and got a yes. Then the pastor used the Bible to show how human hearts are wicked and thus cause people to do the wrong things, and let George read how his own heart could be changed. All of this seemed new to George, so the visit was ended with a prayer but no pressure for a commitment.

Those visits to the jail continued about every other week. During one of them the two prayed together and George asked Jesus to come into his heart. He told the pastor about some other inmates he knew. The staff was getting accustomed to seeing this minister around, and they cooperated in helping him to visit with the other inmates. As the weeks went by, the preacher found himself with quite a "case load" at the jail. A Bible study for inmates was arranged for the mornings, with afternoon counseling sessions set up. He was devoting an entire day to work behind the bars.

When it dawned on him that he had become really involved in jail ministry, he began to look for help. Scanning book catalogs, he found some listed, and bought and devoured them; from their bibliographies, he learned of periodicals that might provide help, and secured some of them. From these resources, he learned much about how a Christian witness is needed in jails and prisons, and some things that could be done to help meet the tremendous needs of inmates.

Then, much to his surprise, the warden contacted him and asked if he would like to be the volunteer Protestant chaplain for the jail. This would mean an opportunity to minister right on the cell blocks and have contact with *all* of the inmates, not just those who had expressed enough interest to respond when called out. After securing church approval for this ministry, the pastor who "went to jail" got locked up with the other sinners there!

I was that pastor!

I reread the materials I had acquired on jail and prison ministry, looking for help. Most materials in print present two points of view: the professional chaplain working full time in the state or federal prison; or the church carrying on a ministry of volunteers in the local jail or prison. But there is practically nothing in print on the unique opportunities opened when the pastor goes to jail. Thus I felt the need to write down some of my experiences and suggestions for a pastoral ministry behind bars.

The first two chapters take a look at the needs in jails and prisons and why a *pastor* is needed to help minister to those needs. There follow chapters on what a pastor can do, how the local church can become involved, widening the jail ministry to include families of inmates, and the importance of follow-up. The final chapter points out that the inmates are not the only persons behind bars who present an opportunity for service. Throughout, names have been changed, and spelling in excerpts from letters has been left as it was in the original.

Decisions for Christ on the cell block, public professions of faith in jail chapel services, baptisms inside the institution, evidences of Christian growth in unfavorable circumstances, grudging approval of skeptical staff members, and continuing correspondence with inmates, both saved and lost, are only a few of the benefits for the pastor who goes to jail.

1
There Are Needs
in There

The ever-increasing numbers of persons in penal institutions are as great a challenge as any for the Christian
ministry. There are fifty federal, six hundred state, and
over five thousand local prisons and jails. On top of that,
there are over eight hundred juvenile institutions, and
the penal system includes work release centers, halfway
houses, work farms, reformatories, prison reception centers, and a variety of other confinement facilities. These
hold less than thirty thousand federal, over two hundred
fifty thousand state, and perhaps three hundred thousand
local inmates. One estimate says that over a million persons pass through American jails in one year![1] The cost to
the taxpayers is said to be over $7 billion annually.[2] That
means that about the same number of people are behind
bars as live in the state of Vermont, and, that a number
of people larger than the population of Houston, Texas,
pass through or are locked up in one of the centers for
detainment every year. Not much imagination is needed
to perceive that those who have run afoul of the law, and
those who are operating these institutions, have many
needs. Space will allow consideration only of those that
have bearing upon Christian ministry.

Two inmates from one institution outlined some of
those needs:

— *The need* to experience normal social contacts with outside groups not only to prepare us for eventual release, but also to help us survive as persons in a prison environment.
— *The need* to have someone listen to our frustrations.
— *The need* for someone to take a personal interest in our family problems and to contact our families when possible.
— *The need* for someone to help us with some of our legal problems, not as lawyers, but as friends who may be able to say a good word for us.[3]

Feelings and emotions inmates may experience give some indication as to their spiritual and psychological needs: bitterness, total bewilderment, abandonment, boredom, loneliness, hostility, fear of safety and of what may lie ahead, hopelessness, and devastation.[4] The environment is dehumanizing, and there is routine and regimentation for all. Even in prison, there is a power structure among the inmates. This power structure in most institutions is aided and abetted by corruption to a greater or lesser degree by the staff in order to hold down violence. It is easy to understand that "there are many paranoias which prisoners experience, like the feeling that walls are closing in or the staring of hands of a clock which seem never to move."[5] One factor often reported by prisoners is the constant noise—radios and TVs blaring, shouting and cursing, even in the wee hours of the morning. And one that is really hard to adjust to is the lack of privacy; no place to get by oneself for review and meditation. To get that quiet some voluntarily choose to spend time in an isolation cell.

Being a Christian does not immunize one from ending up in jail, but though many inmates are church members, most know little or nothing of a personal experience of conversion by saving faith in Jesus Christ. Operating from a spiritual vacuum clouds their perception of their situation and how to adjust to it. The steadying influence of the Scriptures and the comforts of Christian fellowship mean little if anything to them. In fact, not a few, in trying to find a reason for their problems, fix the blame on God for letting them get into such a mess. Those who are believers find themselves in an antagonistic environment, and, if they try to invoke their faith through Bible reading and prayer, are subjected to ridicule and criticism. If they actively witness, they may be subjected to all kinds of harassment and persecution from fellow inmates. All need help in finding the Way.

Anxiety about family is one prevalent inmate worry. Communication with the outside is limited and garbled. Words written in letters have a way of changing meaning, and even hurried telephone conversations have a way of being mistranslated. The personal visits are all too far apart, and under far less than ideal conditions: limited in time, on a phone while looking through glass, with the confusion of others talking at the same time. It all adds up to confusion and depression. There is hurt and guilt because the closest family members have been drawn into the mess. The wife of one inmate said, "People don't realize when a man is sent to prison that the wife is sentenced to serve his time with him."[6] Inmate needs are many and pressing, and offer a unique opportunity for ministry by pastors and churches who want to carry out the commands of the Master.

Inmates are not the only persons in prison. There is also the prison staff: the guards, counselors, and administrative staff. Add to these the lawyers, caseworkers, deputies, and parole and probation officers who come and go, and there are multiplied others whose lives are affected by their contacts with inmates and their families. These people also have psychological and spiritual needs. Their hearts

tend to become hardened as they become calloused by
the unending tales of woe unfolded to them by those
permanently inside the institution. They are beset by ag-
nosticism and skepticism as they experience the inequities and injustices of the "system." They also present a
challenge and opportunity for ministry.

Challenge and Opportunity

To bring the gospel to these more-than-half-a-million
people with such complex needs, there are less than six
hundred full-time chaplains, over five hundred of them
on government payrolls; and that includes chaplains of *all*
persuasions. One author says that fifteen hundred additional chaplains are needed, and that, if provided, they
will have to be funded by the church.[7] Nearly all of the
present full-time chaplains are in state and federal institutions, with little organized ministry for the hundreds of
local and county jails, with populations ranging from eight
or ten to up into the thousands. To adequately fund full-
time ministries at all prisons and jails with their satellites
would require far more money at a time when govern-
ments at all levels are cutting back, and churches do not
have prison ministries as a priority item in their budgets.
The answer to this dilemma is volunteers: pastors and
church members who will give themselves to the task of
taking the gospel to those behind the walls and strength-
ening the faith those who know Him.

The local jail is the place of greatest opportunity, and,
at the same time, it is the most neglected. It is there that
most people find themselves in really serious trouble for
the first time in their lives. Most are young adults: the
average age is twenty-six. Duane Pederson says, "Of
America's correctional institutions, it is the thousands of
jails that confine the most people with the greatest needs

but for whom the least is being done. Yet I believe jails
have the greatest potential ministry within the entire correctional system."8

The jail is different from the prison in many ways. Many
of those in the local lockup have not been tried and sentenced; many are transients, moving from one institution
to another, awaiting new trial or appeal. Inmates may be
under local, state, or federal jurisdiction. Thus, at prisons
things tend to be fairly stable with inmates knowing what
is likely to come when, but the instability at the jail adds
to the uncertainty and anxiety of the prisoners.

One other important factor is present: those inside the
bars at the city or county detention center are people
from the community where the pastor has his ministry. As
he ministers to the needs of inmates, he also presents a
caring witness to their families and friends, and to the
entire community. His "clients" may well be some of his
own parishioners, or those of fellow pastors. As a volunteer, the pastor has unparalleled opportunities for contacts for Christ which would never come to him through
the routine ministries of the church where he serves. One
inmate wrote:

> Fifteen months ago, I started my vacation at this fine
> resort! Down in Intake, I saw a few Bibles, but I wasn't
> going to pick one up and play holy! I've been here before
> and have seen so many become temporarily religious I was
> not going to "cop out."
> I'd seen different ministers come to visit inmates from
> their church. Some to say how embarrassed the congrega-
> tion was at their publicity, some just to say, "Good Luck."
> One day a jovial man came in to pass out a few tracts and
> paperbacks. Some of these books had hardened criminals
> on the cover, get-away driver for Bonnie & Clyde, big
> time cons, etc. The stories were interesting and easy to

read. The end was always the same: the bad guy heard the gospel and became one of *God's children.* I saw these criminals believing and it started me thinking. Next time "Curly" (new inmates called him that) came, I listened a little more to him. He gave me a New Testament, which I started reading when I moved upstairs. It was almost Christmas, so I thought I'd read all four "different versions" of His birth—they weren't different!

I, too, realized how lost I was. It was traumatic to learn how much of a sinner I was, humiliating! I was rebellious, abhorrent, and a vain human who was evil by nature and unworthy of God's grace and mercy and love. On December 10, 1980, I swallowed my pride, admitted defeat, was humbled, repented, and accepted Christ of the Bible—a different Christ than I had pictured before!

What a difference between a churchgoer and a true Bible Christian! I know 'cuz I have been both. Thanks, "Curly"! I guess God used you to get my brain in gear. Thanks for being here.[9]

In the prisons, the long-termers are hardened and suspicious, often drawing newcomers into their perverse ways and increasing the likelihood of the inmate resuming a life of crime and lawlessness upon release. Much is made over rehabilitation programs, but they simply do not work; in fact, when God is left out, they are contrary to God's Word (Luke 5:36; 11:24-26). But "If any man be in Christ, he is a new creature: old things are passed away; behold, all things are become new" (2 Cor. 5:17; see John 3:5-6). While men and women are still young and their hearts are not hardened is the time for them to hear and respond to the Word of God. They have been avoiding the church, and would ridicule attempts to lead them in the right direction while they were on the street. But in the strange, confining, uncertain, and frightening surroundings of the jail, with observations of hardened criminals who are passing through as a result of repetition of their old ways of life, they often become more open to presentations of the Truth.

While jails and prisons are caldrons of evil, many inmates within them are open to the Gospel because of boredom and desperation. Some, when free, were too busy to give Jesus a second thought. Now that they are forced into idleness, they are willing to listen to God's Word—and some will be converted. Other inmates are so desperate that they will try anything, even religion, in the hope that it may help them. Some of these, also, may be converted.

An amazing aspect of the New Testament message is that God does not care what motivates a man to come to Christ. He cares only that the man comes—because when one truly comes to Jesus, he is changed.[10]

A Biblical Mandate

After being arrested by the Lord Jesus Himself on the Damascus Road (see Acts 9), Saul of Tarsus asked, "Lord, what wilt thou have me to do?" (Acts 9:6). When he had further talks with the Lord and learned His will that he be a missionary to the hated Gentiles, *he went!* From His Word, God makes it plain that believers in Christ should go with the message of salvation by grace through faith to the uttermost parts of the earth. Too often the Great Commission is thought of as having application mostly to faraway lands; yet as Luke reported it in Acts 1:8, the witness was to begin (and continue) at home; and to some people, the local jail would indeed be "the uttermost part of the earth"!

Paul wrote to Timothy that "God our Saviour . . . will have all men to be saved, and come to the knowledge of the truth" (1 Tim. 2:3-4), and Peter said that He "is long-suffering to us-ward, not willing that any should perish, but that all should come to repentance" (2 Pet. 3:9). God told His prophet Ezekiel that he would be held accountable for those whom he failed to warn of impending judgment (Ezek. 33:1-9). There are multiplied thousands inside jail and prison walls who have never heard of the coming judgment or the pardon that is available to them.

> If thou forbear to deliver them that are drawn unto death, and those that are ready to be slain; If thou sayest, Behold, we knew it not; doth not he that pondereth the heart consider it? and he that keepeth thy soul, doth he not know it? and shall not he render to every man according to his works (Prov. 24:11-12)?

While this Scripture may have general application, there are some specific references to prisoners in others. The writer of Hebrews admonished, "Remember those in prison as if you were their fellow prisoners, and those who are mistreated as if you yourselves were suffering" (Heb. 13:3, NIV). Jesus, who taught that one phase of His ministry was to preach deliverance to the captives or prisoners (Luke 4:18-19) said that when judgment day comes, one of the criteria which will demonstrate that one has trusted Him will be the visiting of those in prison (Matt. 25:31-46; note vv. 36,40,43-44).

Summary

There is a great field in America's correctional institutions waiting to be harvested, but the laborers are too few. They are also concentrated at one end of that field, in the state and federal prisons. The field of the local jail has the fewest workers. It is a great opportunity to reinforce community witness and ministry, and the potential of producing fruit which will increase thirtyfold, sixtyfold, and a hundredfold as inmates find Christ and then influence other inmates, family members, and friends. The Bible reveals the concern of Jesus for those behind bars, commands that they be ministered to, and warns that failure to bring the message to them will be one of the criteria at the judgment. The key to service in the local jail is the pastor, serving on a consistent volunteer basis himself in obedience to the biblical mandate.

Notes

1. Duane Pederson, *How to Establish a Jail and Prison Ministry* (Nashville: Thomas Nelson Publishers, 1979), p. 20.

2. Frank Constantino, *Crime Fighter* (Dallas: Acclaimed Books, 1981) p. xv.

3. Paul Schoonmaker, *The Prison Connection* (Valley Forge, Pa.: Judson Press, 1978), p. 14.

4. Author's personal notes, Correctional Chaplaincy Course, Arlington, Va., January, 1981.

5. *Prison People, A Guide for Prison Fellowship Volunteers* (Washington: Prison Fellowship, 1981), p. 21.

6. Constantino, p. 101.

7. Dale K. Pace, *A Christian's Guide to Effective Jail and Prison Ministries* (Old Tappan, N.J.: Fleming H. Revell, 1976), p. 34.

8. Pederson, p. 49.

9. Personal letter to author.

10. Pace, p. 40.

2
Why Me, Lord?

The tremendous need, the great challenge, and the golden opportunity presented by the local jail call for a pastor to allot scarce, precious time to a volunteer, personal ministry behind those bars. Jesus said, "Ye have not chosen me, but I have chosen you, and ordained you, that ye should go and bring forth fruit, and that your fruit should remain" (John 15:16). It is clear from His teachings that this "fruit" is not necessarily budgets, buildings, and baptisms. The *fruit* comes from sowing the seed, even in what may appear to some to be unlikely fields (see Matt. 13:3-9; 18-23). The pastor, with a call to serve, training, and experience, is the most qualified to sow, cultivate, fertilize, and weed this fertile field so that there will be a great harvest.

A Pastor Needs to Go to Jail!

John's recording of the Great Commission says simply, "As my Father hath sent me, even so send I you" (20:21). When Jesus began His public ministry, He had an opportunity to speak in His hometown synagogue at Nazareth (Luke 4:16-19). He read from Isaiah 61:1-2,

The spirit of the Lord God is upon me; because the Lord hath anointed me to preach good tidings to the meek; he

hath sent me to bind up the brokenhearted, to proclaim
liberty to the captives, and the opening of the prison to
them that are bound; To proclaim the acceptable year of
the Lord

He then told the home folks that He had come to fulfil
that Scripture. Theologians may argue that "captives"
and "them that are bound" refer to those in the clutches
of sin and not to prison inmates; yet who else are more in
the grip of Satan? If Jesus understood His ministry to be
to such, so also ought everyone whom He has chosen and
ordained!

The apostle Paul wrote to the Corinthians, "Though I
be free from all men, yet have I made myself servant unto
all, that I might gain the more" (1 Cor. 9:19). He outlined
his approach to people in different walks of life and persuasions, adding, "I am made all things to all men, that I
might by all means save some" (v. 22). Far too many want
to serve God on *their* terms and not *His*. Like Isaiah, they
may respond to His call by saying, "Here am I, send me,"
and then add, "but not to the jail, or rescue mission, or
inner city, or Timbucktu."

It was said of Jesus that He was the friend of publicans
and sinners. He associated with such despicable people as
the hated tax-collectors, Matthew and Zacchaeus, an un-
named woman with a very tarnished reputation at a well
outside of Sychar in Samaria and another out of whom He
had cast seven demons, laid hands on "unclean" lepers
and paralytics, and accepted a condemned criminal who
was dying with Him on a neighboring cross.

For verily he took not on him the nature of angels; but
he took on him the seed of Abraham. Wherefore in all
things it behoved him to be made like unto his brethren,
that he might be a merciful and faithful high priest in

things pertaining to God, to make reconciliation for the sins of the people. For in that he himself hath suffered being tempted, he is able to succour them that are tempted (Heb. 2:16-18).

Jesus was all things to all men, even enduring temptation, so that He might minister to all. A pastor should be willing to go where the people in need are, to share with them His love and compassion.

Serving in a county jail is good medicine for pride, one of Satan's major tools and a potent pitfall for every minister. Jesus taught that the way to the top of the heap is to deliberately seek the bottom, (Matt. 20:25-28) and He demonstrated it by humbly washing the feet of the disciples. He said, "I have given you an example, that ye should do as I have done to you. Verily, verily, I say unto you, the servant is not greater than his lord; neither he that is sent greater than he that sent him" (John 13:15-16). In the same vein, Paul admonished, "For I say, through the grace given unto me, to every man that is among you, not to think of himself more highly than he ought to think, but to think soberly, according as God hath dealt to every man the measure of faith" (Rom. 12:3).

The world may conclude that a pastor's ministry gets better exposure through service club activities and honorary doctorates because of philanthropic activities. Or, it might be easy to conclude that real service is serving in the ecclesiastical hierarchy, and thus getting recognition and promotion to better positions in more prestigious locations. Serving in the local jail will help a pastor to keep all these things in proper focus.

There is so much to be learned at Hardknocks University! Seminary classes and special courses may prepare one for duty, but there is no substitute for being in the spot where the water hits the wheel.

One day I walked onto the cell block, and was immediately accosted by two inmates. "Whatcha got there?"

"Oh, some books from Chaplain Ray and some New Testaments."

"How about coming over here to our cell? We want to talk to you a minute."

There was a little apprehension, but inside the cell, one said, "Say, I read that book—boy, the Lord really worked that guy over, didn't He?"

The other added, "Yeah. I read this one here. That guy went through all I've been through and then some, and yet God saved him. Rev, how does a man get saved anyway?"

It is one thing to read about such experiences or to hear about them from others, but it is something else to be a part of them! Inside those walls are men and women for whom someone has been praying, and whom the Lord has been preparing. To be sure, some will never listen to the preacher; others will "fence" with him, maybe even try to embarrass him in an effort to gain Brownie points with peers. These experiences help the minister to sharpen his tools for use inside and outside the walls, to evaluate and reevaluate his resources and approaches, to really witness!

At Jerusalem, Jesus saw a man who had been born blind. The disciples got into a discussion as to why he was that way: environment, or inheritance? But Jesus responded to the need by giving the man his sight. Later, when some of the religious authorities questioned the man, he said that he didn't really know anything about the theological implications, but one thing was perfectly clear: "One thing I know, that, whereas I was blind, now I see (John 9:25). Seeing was believing for him! When the pastor works inside the prison, those who are spiritually blind receive sight, and one's own faith is strengthened.

> Since, then, we know what it is to fear the Lord, we try to persuade men. What we are is plain to God, and I hope it is also plain to your conscience. We are not trying to commend ourselves to you again, but are giving you an opportunity to take pride in us, so that you can answer those who take pride in what is seen rather than in what is in the heart. If we are out of our mind, it is for the sake of God; if we are in our right mind, it is for you. For Christ's love compels us, because we are convinced that one died for all, and therefore all died. And he died for all, that those who live should no longer live for themselves but for him who died for them and was raised again (2 Cor. 5:11-15, NIV).

Paul wrote that there were two factors compelling him to share the gospel message: the fear of the Lord, and the love of Christ. Every pastor works under the same compulsions. He remembers the warnings of Jesus about the realities of hell (Mark 9:43-48; Luke 16:19-31), and Bible testimonies of His sacrificial love (Gal. 2:21; Rev. 1:5), and must tell others of both the severity and goodness of God. In the jails are people with hearts that have been broken and hardened; people who have been discarded and forgotten by society, but not by God. The preacher who needs to give can find behind those walls and bars those who need to receive. Yes, a pastor needs to go to jail!

Inmates Need a Pastor

> And they were scattered, because there is no shepherd: and they became meat to all the beasts of the field, when they were scattered. My sheep wandered through all the mountains, and upon every high hill: yea, my flock was

scattered upon all the face of the earth, and none did search or seek after them (Ezek. 34:5-6).

No shepherd, no one seeking or searching for the sheep who were scattered and lost, God says. This indictment is certainly true in local jails, where many an inmate could say, "I looked on my right hand, and beheld, but there was no man that would know me: refuge failed me; no man cared for my soul" (Ps. 142:4). Like sheep, most of the lost do not know that they are lost. But a society that has concluded that those who are behind bars are getting what they deserve has ignored or forgotten them. But even if they don't know of their need for a shepherd, and many rebel and react negatively to being shepherded, the need is still there. Let an inmate speak:

> I just wanted to drop you a note this cold Sunday morning to express my thanks and eternal gratitude to you for your visits and comforts during my recent stay at Erie Co. prison. Those visits to my cell on Wed. afternoon and our talks helped me a great deal.
>
> I am now at Western and still reading the New Testament you gave me in your last visit to me. I wouldn't let it out of my possion [sic] for anything in the world.
>
> We have a Prot. chaplain here. I've seen him once in a group when I filled out a form. That may be his way—my way is your way. I vividly remember the only sermon it was my priviledge to hear you preach, "Your Sin Will Find You Out."
>
> Reverend—I see that every day down here. Some of the results are not pretty to see or hear about. A "stabbing" of an informer never is.[1]

The sad truth is that some prisons and nearly all jails have no chaplains, and many have no religious services at all. A 1972 survey by the Law Enforcement Assistance

Association revealed that 42 percent of local jails do not have any religious services—meaning that inmates in as many as two thousand institutions are not being ministered to.[2] Wardens, sheriffs, and jailers for the most part welcome such ministry once they see that it will present little disruption for them and will help occupy the prisoners' time.

A pastor ministering on a regular basis inside the jail has a unique advantage. A large number of people (not all of them inside the walls) feel that preachers are in it just for the money, and that they won't get involved in anything that doesn't pay off. A paid, or staff, chaplain is sometimes regarded with skepticism and suspicion because he is assumed to be a part of the "establishment," maybe even a "snitch" or informer. Many paid chaplains don't get the chance to prove they can be trusted. When it gets through to inmates that the chaplain is there because he wants to be, and because he is concerned about and interested in them, he begins to get open ears and affirmative responses that would not be possible otherwise. He can do a job that no one else can do! One inmate told me, "Others come in here on Sundays and preach to us, and what they say is OK, but we never see them any other time. It's like they're just doing their job and getting credit for it, but they don't really care for us." When Jesus "saw the multitudes, he was moved with compassion on them, because they fainted, and were scattered abroad, as sheep having no shepherd" (Matt. 9:36). The pastor who really cares reflects this love and compassion of the Master, and even the most hardened can see Him as the man of God gives himself to the brokenhearted, the captives, and those who are bound.

Thanks be unto God for dedicated church members who become burdened for those in jails and prisons and take steps to minister to them. It can be demonstrated by testimonies that these ministries have been effective. Yet most ministries in the local jail are conducted on a volunteer, "round-robin" basis, with a different person conducting worship services each time they are held, and with little or no further contact with the prisoners. If there are Bible studies, still different persons hold them, and there is usually no coordination between the various efforts. That badly needed personal touch is missing, and so is the continuity that makes possible the establishment of a basis for familiarity and trust upon which relationships can be built.

As noted earlier, the jail atmosphere is that of uncertainty and insecurity; there is constant change; yet there is also a depressing sameness. Inmates find it difficult to really relate to a new face and a new personality every week. A pastor who will devote one day a week to jail ministry will help to provide some stability to an unstable situation, a point of reference to those who are scattered abroad as sheep having no shepherd. As he comes regularly, a familiar face with a friendly smile, those who are drawn into their shells can begin to feel that here is someone who can listen to their anxieties and frustrations, give them an opportunity to unload; and, when they receive a sympathetic ear, they are more likely to give one themselves.

A volunteer chaplaincy in the local jail which includes a chapel service will also give prisoners an opportunity to hear systematic presentation of Bible truths. Where there is no coordination of different speakers, it is likely that prisoners will hear messages on John 3:16 and the prodigal son over and over. When one pastor speaks to them regularly, he can minister to both old and new believers, as well as bring evangelistic messages. Thus he provides opportunity for growth as well as for spiritual birth.

I am speaking for myself as well as a few other men when I tell you how we enjoyed your sermon last night. Through your sermon last night, God has helped me realize how wrong I have been in a few areas; like, for a long time now I have strongly believed that once a person accepts Jesus Christ as their Savior and believe what the Bible teaches about Christian living and about praising God, there wasent any real need to go to church. But thanks to the Lord, he reveald to me through your sermon how wrong I was. I now realize how very important going to church realy is to a growing Christen. You see, I have had some questions that have been poping up for a long time now that I could not seem to find the answers to, so I prayed every day that God would reveal the answers to me, and you want to know something, he more than answered my questions. He not only answered my prayers through your sermon, but your sermon served to show me the importance of attending church. So I believe now that God realy does answer prayers.[3]

The psalmist said, "Before I was afflicted, I went astray, but now have I kept thy word. It is good for me that I have been afflicted; that I might learn thy statutes. I know, O Lord, that thy judgments are right, and that thou in faithfulness hast afflicted me" (Ps. 119:67,71,75). Of course, the affliction of imprisonment is nearly always self-inflicted; yet it would not occur if God did not permit it. Some seem to get away with the worst crimes without incarceration. They have connections in the right places and enough resources to stay out of jail. Others who don't know the right people and live from hand to mouth can't even get out on bail when picked up for some relatively minor offense. In the local jail are many who are in serious trou-

ble for the first time in their lives. They left God out, or
just paid lip service to Him; now they need Him.

In every lockup, there are plenty of "jail-house lawyers" (inmates who think they are lawyers), yet, thank
God, not too many preachers. The one just recently admitted is confused and scared. He has no idea which, if
any, of his fellow inmates to trust or confide in. He needs
someone from "on the street" to confide in, to unload on.
A pastor who is compassionate and sympathetic can fill
this need and help him to get his confused picture into
focus, often just by listening. Maybe he is in there because
no one would listen to him before.

And there are some who, when reviewing their lives,
realize that everything they have tried has not brought
the satisfaction or peace they were looking for, and now
they are ready to hear about who Jesus is and what He can
do for them.

> Hi! I'll bet you surprised to hear from me after all this
> time, but I just wanted you to know that I did appreciate
> your introducing me to Christ. I know that it proabley
> seamed like I wasn't interested to learn, but I was. It was
> just that I had to get honest with myself, ya know that it
> was hard for me to admit to myself that I was haveing
> problems with my life that I couldn't solve, and that I
> needed help.
>
> I was one of those people that thinks they are able to do
> whatever they want, you know, the tough guy that doesn't
> want or need any help. I know that I have done a lot of
> things to hurt other people, fighting and robine houses,
> and I also know that I can't change my past, but . . . I know
> that God has forgiven me for what I have done.
>
> Although I still don't go to church, I do have a personal
> relationship with Christ. When I'm alone in my cell at
> night we talk and I ask God to lead me through these hard

times, and to help make me a better person. I know God is with me and helping me a lot. I can realy see my aditude changeing. When I first got put in jail I was resentful against everyone besides me. I know in my heart that the policeman that shot me was trying to take my life away. I was very bitter because of that but now with the help of God I have learned to forgive. Like I said, I can't change my past, but I know I can look forward to a better future.[4]

To Sum It Up

The most effective ministry in the local jail can be carried out by the pastor who sees the need, the challenge, and the opportunity. He is the one who is called and equipped to reach and minister to inmates. He actually needs such a ministry to follow in the steps of Jesus and Paul, as inoculation against pride, as an invaluable source of experience, and as an outlet for his Spirit-impelled compassion.

And jail inmates need a pastor, too. Many jails don't have any kind of ministry, and most don't have the services of an experienced pastor to listen to and counsel with their clientele. Inmates need systematic presentation of the Word which a pastor can provide, and many who are in trouble for the first time in their lives are now ready and need to hear about the Savior.

"The harvest truly is plenteous, but the laborers are few; Pray ye therefore the Lord of the harvest, that he will send forth labourers into his harvest" (Matt. 9:37-38).

Notes

1. Personal letter to author.
2. Duane Pederson, *How to Establish a Jail and Prison Ministry.* (Nashville: Thomas Nelson Publishers, 1979), p. 23.
3. Personal letter to author.
4. Personal letter to author.

3
Here I Am—
What Do I Do?

The need for pastoral ministry in local jails is over-whelming. What can a pastor do, once he gets a vision of the fertile field and the urgent need for it to be worked?

Motivation

Before getting into it, the preacher will do well to check what is moving him to become involved. There are wrong motives, and there are right motives for going to jail.

Guilt and sympathy stir some people. They actually hate to see someone locked up, and have the idea that a society that does not understand is making them suffer. They know what is wrong with the inmates and the system, and have all the answers. They soon turn the inmates off and drop out. Others want their peers to admire them and feel that working in jail can be a way to show them how committed they are. It would be well to remember what Jesus said in the Sermon on the Mount about displays of religious piosity (Matt. 6:1-4). Cons can spot a phony pretty quickly, and when they realize that the visitors don't really care for them, may just tell them not to bother.

Some have a romantic fascination with crime and criminals, and want to experience the notoriety that comes from associating with infamous ones. This novelty soon wears off, and they lose interest.

And then there are those who get into the work solely to boast about how many they have won to the Lord. Most inmates resent a pushy approach. It either turns them off, or they will make a "decision" just to get the eager one off their backs.[1]

Ex-con Frank Constantino says,

> Who should be a volunteer prison minister? Only those who are called of God to this particular work. Why? Just as everyone is not called to the mission fields of Africa, to a church leadership position, or to the tents of evangelism, so it is with prison ministry.[2]

He adds,

> The question of a calling is most essential in any work for the Lord, the foundation on which everything else is built. Remember, in all works for God there are going to be hard times as well as blessings. Through the hard times it is going to be the sureness of your calling that will sustain you, even when everything seems to be going wrong.[3]

Whom the Lord calls, He equips and empowers as they yield themselves to Him. There is nothing glamorous or easy about working in the jail, but having God in charge, while not eliminating obstacles and distractions, will surely be a source of courage and direction (see Josh. 1:9).

One other ingredient should be emphasized: love for inmates. To the world they are lawbreakers, rebellious, violent, profane, defiant, and deserving of what they are getting. And all these things may indeed be true. Yet those who would minister effectively must see them through the Lord's eyes: "God commendeth his love toward us, in that, while we were yet sinners, Christ died for us" (Rom. 5:8). His love to persons is not because they deserve it, but because they need it. So it is with those behind bars. Plagued with resentment, bitterness, and guilt, they need someone to love them just as they are, who will, with loving words and actions, point them to Jesus Christ, Who is the Author and Perfecter of authentic love.[4]

Prison worker Duane Pederson says, "I believe that the only lasting and honest motive for a Christian must be obedience to Christ, including the desire to see Him honored and the wish to meet the needs of inmates in a sensitive, caring way."[5]

Qualifications

With the right motivation in clear focus, a pastor should examine his qualifications. The "congregation" in jail is not the same as that which meets Sunday mornings in the sanctuary, and the pastor who goes to jail should be aware of some critical criteria for effective ministry, both in jail and on the church field, but especially in jail.

First, there must be commitment to the task. Jail work is not for the fad-chaser who works at one ministry today and another next week. Gaining the confidence and trust of jail staff and inmates requires a demonstration of dedication in the face of obstacles and frustrations that many times have been developed just to see what the worker is made of. Becoming familiar with jail environment, rules, and learning to relate to inmates takes time and effort, often beyond what would be required in other situations. Those who start and stop demoralize the inmates, disappoint and disillusion the staff, and mar their image to the community. Consistency, persistence, and patience are primary virtues.

Willingness to work under authority is important. Rules

and procedures which may seem silly and nonproductive
to the novice have been distilled out of years of constant
contact with prison inmates. The pastor may conclude
that God is his authority, and that he needn't observe
these inane restrictions. And he won't have to, either,
because he'll find himself ministering in some place other
than the jail. Most of those practices are designed to protect staff, volunteers, and the inmates themselves. With
the passing of time, the preacher will understand the
"why" of most of them.

> A prison ministry is no place for a novice Christian. You
> should know what you believe and why, and should be
> able to explain it in a clear, understandable way for people
> who have little church background. Inmates aren't above
> asking tough theological questions, and you should not be
> intimidated or humiliated by such encounters.[6]

A mature, well-grounded faith which is backed up by
thorough knowledge of the Scriptures is essential for the
pastor who will be in an atmosphere of skepticism and
agnoticism away from the security of his library. What
Paul wrote to Timothy, "Study to shew thyself approved
unto God, a workman that needeth not to be ashamed,
rightly dividing the word of truth," (2 Tim. 2:15), really is
pertinent at this point. You will do well to have your
convictions in order about such things as suicide, abortion,
adultery, incest, drugs, and drunkenness. It will not be
very long before you will have to defend them.

A word of caution: when denominational questions
come up which could cause confusion and differences
among inmates, it is wise to simply say, "Yes, I belong to
a church, but I am here representing Jesus Christ, and I
don't want you to get Him confused with any church,
because He is Lord of them all."

While the pastor who goes to jail should be thoroughly grounded in his faith, he should also at the same time be open and teachable. He may have a Th.D. degree and years of experience in the pastorate, but every day in jail is a new experience unlike anything he has encountered before. He can learn about inmates from both the staff and inmates. He can gain new insight into Bible truths from them, too, especially as they apply to that unique environment. It does not take the know-it-all who goes to serve in the jail very long to find out how little he does know!

Many wonder what they are going to say to inmates or staff members, when the truth is that many times it is not necessary to say anything. To be effective in jail ministry, the pastor must be a good listener. That is difficult for someone who talks as much as some preachers like to do, but active listening will communicate concern and interest to the prisoner, and open doors for witnessing and sharing Christ.

> Inmates don't need someone to talk to them as much as they need someone to listen. They don't need to be condemned or preached at. Most realize all too well how badly they have messed up their lives. They need a concerned, supportive friend who will sit with them and just listen as they talk and think out loud.[7]

It is vitally important that the pastor who would reach men and women in jail for Christ should accept them as persons. It is not necessary to accept their deeds or lifestyle to accept *them;* but if they are to be ministered to, they must be taken just like they are. The preacher must sincerely say, "There, but for the grace of God, go I," and put aside judgment to accept the person of the inmate as being of ultimate worth and value in God's sight.

"Have you met Bill Johnson?" the range boss asked.

"No, I don't think so," was my reply.

"C'mon back here, then," he said. Bill had been in the papers and on television for the past several weeks.

"Say, whatcha doin' in here?" It was unusual for somebody in civvies to be on the cell block.

"Well, the warden asked me to be the Protestant chaplain awhile back, so I'm in here trying to tell everybody that Jesus loves them and wants them to be in heaven with Him."

"Howzit goin? Is anybody getting saved?"

"Yes, there have been a few decisions." Nothing was said about his legal or criminal situation, though it had received wide publicity, and was not pretty. He had received a New Testament a week earlier, and said that he had been reading it.

"That's great," he responded. "Can I be your next customer?" He was! (Bill Johnson is not his real name; he has since been baptized inside the jail, and has been instrumental in at least two other inmates' decisions for Christ.)

And the pastor who goes to jail must be dependable and consistent. Inmates have known so many broken promises that they rarely expect anyone to be dependable. Though they may let him down and disappoint him, they expect the Christian worker to be faithful and reliable. They have to develop a thick veneer of distrust to survive in jail, and the preacher cannot afford to let his relationships with them end in further failure and rejection. When promises are made, they should be kept; and when they are, an inmate is a little less suspicious, a little more open. Playing favorites will also compromise witness, so the jail minister must be careful to see that all are accorded the same attention and service, where possible.[8]

Preparation

If motives and qualifications are in order, a pastor will do well to put in some preparation time before getting involved in the jail. There are both personal and administrative steps to be taken.

The first step in personal preparation is prayer, communication with the Lord. Pederson says, "This starts, I believe, with soul-searching prayer that seeks answers to questions like: Is this a ministry I should explore further? Do I see the need and feel a burden for those in prison?"9 Prayer time should include praise to God, and confession and forsaking of known sins. Requests should be made for direction (Prov. 3:5-6) and wisdom (Jas. 1:5), for doors to open to the jail through the administration, and for inmates to be prepared by the Holy Spirit to receive the gospel message, and for His guidance to those who have been so prepared.

Then, there is the need for study. First of all, *Bible* study. The pastor should use his Bible dictionary, concordance, reference Bible, Hebrew and Greek to become familiar with passages of Scripture about imprisonment and prisoners. He should be up to date on a *simple* presentation of how to get right with God. The average inmate could care less about the latest theological fad or denominational emphasis, but he does need to hear a clear message about Christ crucified, buried, risen again, and demonstrating His power in the lives of those who trust Him. Bible answers to frequently asked questions like "Where did Cain get his wife?" should be reviewed. Needless to say, the pastor should read the Bible systematically every day for spiritual food and strength as he plans to invade enemy territory in the jail (2 Tim. 3:16-17).

> This book of the law shall not depart out of thy mouth;
> but thou shalt meditate therein day and night, that thou
> mayest observe to do according to all that is written there-
> in: for then thou shalt make thy way prosperous, and then
> shalt thou have good success (Josh. 1:8).

"Meditate upon these things; give thyself wholly to them; that thy profiting may appear to all" (1 Tim. 4:15). There is a sad neglect of meditation in these days of free-ways and pell-mell rushing from one appointment to another. Preachers have forgotten God's commandment to "Be still, and know that I am God" (Ps. 46:10); yet real understanding and comprehension of the Scriptures come only when one waits on God. Meditation is vital in the preparation for jail ministry.

Study should also include materials which will give a general understanding of the criminal justice system so that the minister will be able to respond when inmates bring these matters up. If the jail has a manual it, too, should be gone over. Other books on jail and prison ministry should be reviewed, along with periodicals and pamphlets on the subject. Group study opportunities, such as the Correctional Chaplaincy Course offered annually by the Good News Mission in Arlington, Virginia, afford interchanges with others who are involved with inmates.

Then there is administrative preparation. Depending on the size of the jail, the concurrence and cooperation of the sheriff, warden, and/or jailer must be secured. Checks must be made with ministerial associations to make certain there is not conflict or overlapping; seek to learn what ministries, if any, are already in progress, and if there is any coordination. Arrange for a tour of the jail and to meet personnel. The pastor should be prepared to answer questions about how he plans to conduct the ministry inside the jail. Upon learning what guidelines must be followed, New Testaments, books, and tracts should be ordered for distribution. A special business card for inmates which identifies the minister but does not call attention to his particular church can be helpful. His preparation should include learning all that he can about the institution, the staff, and the inmates.

The pastor who goes to jail will need to make adequate spiritual and administrative preparation to do an effective job.

Activation

There is an old story of the football team that received the opening kickoff to begin the game. At the first and ten, they went back into the huddle and stayed. They were penalized for delay of game, and still they remained in the huddle. After a couple more such infractions and penalties, the officials ruled that they had forfeited the game because they would not come up to the line of scrimmage and play. Just so, there are many who talk a lot about the needs in prisons and jails; they read books and periodicals about the challenge and opportunity; they may even attend courses and seminars, and have conferences with those who are actively involved. But they never get around to actually going and doing. It may sound elementary, but an effective jail ministry means actually being in there and relating to the inmates and staff. Here are some "Do's" and "Don'ts" for the preacher who gets involved in the local lockup.

Do's

Do visit! Many inmates have been written off by family and friends and are never visited by anyone. It is not necessary to discuss their case or the legal system; sports, the weather, politics—all of the barbershop topics (with certain ethical limitations) can open lines of communication and reveal to the inmate an ongoing interest.[10]

Do learn names. Jesus left an ordinance so that men would remember Him, and a dying thief on an adjacent cross asked Him, "Remember me." There is a rapid turnover in jails, yet some inmates are there long enough that in time names can be associated with their faces. They are favorably impressed when the worker demonstrates his personal interest by taking the trouble to learn who they are. Some are there because of acts they performed to gain the attention they felt they were due but not getting. It will be worth the preacher's while to take one of those "How to Make Friends" courses so that he can learn techniques to help him remember names. If the Holy Spirit makes an impression about a particular prisoner, his identity may be secured from another inmate or a guard. Of course, the person in question can always be asked. Like some banks advertise, "Where you are a name and not a number," the prisoner likes to be remembered for who he is, and not by his number or what he is charged with.

Do listen! This has already been said, but it is so important that it needs to be repeated at this point. According to Pederson,

> Many inmates have never had anyone seriously listen to them and really *hear* them. Perhaps the most valuable gift you can bring to an inmate is the quality of being a good listener. By "good" I mean non-judgmental and understanding (although not always believing or accepting everything told you). Be willing to help the inmate find the right questions to ask before you rush in with "answers," even Christian ones.[11]

Listening enables the inmate to vent his feelings, to get

them out where he can look at them objectively, and thus may open the door for presentation of Christ and Bible counsel.

Do pray with inmates at crisis times. Particularly significant to them are the days immediately following incarceration; court appearances; days just before release; hospitalization or death of family members; and negative responses from spouses. These crisis times also provide opportunity for pointing them to pertinent Scriptures and recommending the Bible as a source of strength and guidance, and open the door later for a presentation of the gospel.

Do share a personal testimony of conversion to Christ. Avoid use of "churchy" words like *justification, salvation,* and *regeneration.* An effective testimony is one that tells what life was like before meeting Christ, how the encounter with Jesus took place, and what life has been like since He came into your life. There need be no lurid details of the "before" life; the shorter the testimony, the more effective it can be. "Preaching" should be carefully avoided and reserved for chapel services. Inmates who have been subjected to lectures from spouses, policemen, guards, counselors, judges, and even fellow inmates, are not likely to be interested in ministerial exhortations; they will be turned off. But they do listen to personal experiences with interest.

Do, within administrative bounds, distribute Bibles, New Testaments, Gospels of John, and other Scripture portions, along with books, magazines, and tracts. Modern-language translations that do not compromise basic Bible truths should be included, especially those which use a limited vocabulary that can be understood by those who have reading problems. These materials may be secured at reasonable cost from Bible societies and prison-ministry organizations, and placed in jail libraries (where there is one), in addition to being handed out to inmates. Good reading material is scarce in jail and is eagerly devoured. As the pastor makes regular visits, inmates begin to look forward to receiving materials he brings, and seeds are sown. Many an inmate, bored with TV, radio, cards, and slick magazines, has turned to the Word and come under conviction:

Fred was lying on his bunk, reading a New Testament. I commented, "That's a good book you're into there."

"Yeah, I'm getting a lot out of it. First time I've ever read it. Man, I've gotta do something to get my life straightened out! Not only have I botched it up for myself being in here, but it's hard on the wife, with one kid already here and another one on the way."

I asked if he'd like for me to show him from the book he was holding what he needed to do.

"That'd be great!" he responded. And the seed that had been sowed bore fruit as he prayed, asking the Lord to come into his heart.

Caution: Not only should the approval of the administration be secured, but also it is wise that correctional officers on duty see, and perhaps even check, what is being passed on to inmates. It is not unheard of for contraband to get into the jail and for Christian workers to be blamed.

Do, where permissible and practical, begin a cassette tape ministry. When something is handed to many inmates to read, they may say, "I lost my glasses," or, "My specs got broke before I came in here." What they are really saying is that they have problems with reading. For many, their legal problems have come about because of inability to read well enough to hold a good job. It follows that they cannot read the Bible or Christian literature they receive. But "faith cometh by hearing, and hearing by the word of God" (Rom. 10:17). The entire Bible on cassette tapes is available in not only the King James Version, but modern translations, and is eagerly received by many prisoners. Tapes of sermons by well-known preachers, Bible studies, subjects of interest to those behind bars, are all available if there are resources to secure them.

Do conduct a regular chapel service at a time when it is convenient for the inmates. The writer found that the early Sunday morning chapel service was not well attended because most of the men were still asleep. With the approval of the jail administration, a weeknight service at 8:45 PM was begun, and attendance rose to 25 percent of the jail population, with public decisions for Christ at nearly every service. The visitation, witnessing, and counseling in the cell blocks bears fruit in the worship service, and the pastor who does all these things is able to systematically present the gospel with a new message each time. Men who have grown tired of hearing about the prodigal son, John 3:16, and other messages usually brought at prison chapel services become interested as other passages of the Bible are used. Also, there are more believers in jail than many realize, and the chapel affords the preacher an opportunity to feed them and help them to grow in the Lord. A lively service becomes the topic of discussion on the cell block, and creates interest for the next visit there by the minister.

The jail chapel service may be just like that in the church, if there is a place to hold it. Music is important, and inmates join lustily in singing familiar hymns. They are especially appreciative of solos, duets, and special music presentations. Many inmates bring their Bibles and take notes on the messages, and the pastor will find that as he visits on the cell blocks, questions will come from them, indicating they have listened to his message. Within security considerations, an invitation should be extended to make public profession of faith in Christ or to ask for guidance.

Do conduct a Bible study when time and conditions permit. If a pastor devotes one day to jail ministry and the institution has a large population, he will find it difficult to do this fairly. Frequently, others are working in the jail and leading in Bible studies, so efforts should be made to see that there is no duplication and that everything is coordinated.

Do abide by the rules and procedures of the institution. This, too, has already been said, but it needs to be repeated. The pastor who goes to jail should know what these are, and how they apply to him. *When in doubt, ask!*

> The cardinal rule of prison and jail ministry is to obey all the rules of the institution. You are a guest in someone else's house, so come as a guest. Recognize that each institution is a highly structured community and that security is a primary consideration. . . . There will be many things you will not understand at first, and even after you have been involved in prison or jail ministry for a while you will encounter new situations. Never assume anything; ask questions of those in authority.[12]

Don'ts

Don't take anything in or out.

Even seemingly innocent things can cause great difficulty. In federal prisons, for example, "contraband" is defined as "any article which is unauthorized under the circumstances and includes but is not limited to the following: letters, stamps, food, weapons, tools, implements, messages, and instruments." A stick of gum can be used to make a compression mold of a lock. A simple request to "mail this letter to my mother so it will go out faster" could actually be part of a blackmail effort. . . . Many inmates will try to "con" volunteers and "use" them, so caution is always the rule.[13]

Don't deliver items or messages from inmate to inmate. If they cannot do this through normal channels, then the administration has good reasons for not permitting it.

Don't get involved in inmate arguments. The wise minister will say that he is on both persons' sides (even though he may not be); that his primary concern is that they know the peace that passes all understanding which is available to them in Christ Jesus.

Don't argue about Scripture, or anything else. The argument can be won, and a possible friend and convert lost. Witnessing for Christ while arguing is almost impossible.

Don't be shocked by what you hear.

You are dealing with people who have participated in situations completely alien to your own experience. Be ready to hear anything. That doesn't mean you should allow a prisoner to be lewd or extremely descriptive in sharing or confessing. Many times you cannot avoid hearing something as such, but don't let him know you are shocked, and don't you be offended. Explain to the individual about God's mercy and love, and His ability to "forgive and forget."[14]

Don't take personally an inmate's refusal to listen. Jesus is a gentleman; He will not go where He is not wanted.

Don't judge or condemn inmates, administration, or families. Media accounts are not always accurate and are frequently biased. Information from other inmates is frequently incomplete and slanted. Even what the pastor hears with his own ears and sees with his own eyes still may convey a distorted picture. It is well to keep in mind the words of the Lord Jesus, "Judge not, that ye be not judged. For with what judgment ye judge, ye shall be judged: and with what measure ye mete, it shall be measured to you again" (Matt. 7:1-2). Word that the pastor has criticized one inmate to another will spread quickly and compromise his witness. Guards who learn that they have been put down before prisoners may make things tough for the preacher who is trying to serve during their shift. The jail administrator who finds he has been condemned, whether justly or not, may well decide that it is time for this kind of ministry in his institution to end.

Don't "make waves," regardless of what is seen or heard. To be sure, there are many inequities and shortcomings in the criminal justice system, and not a few may be found in the jail. But it is not the preacher's job to make changes, but rather to bring the Word to inmate and staff. He may well call attention to these needs to others, but should not compromise his mission by getting involved himself.

Don't get "conned." In many ways, ministers tend to be quite naive, and can unwittingly be drawn into seemingly innocent but actually harmful situations. One inmate said to me, "My girl friend is in the hopsital. Wonder if you'd mind checking on her if you happen to be in there?" That's the kind of thing a pastor can do. But before I left the cell block, I was accosted by another inmate who advised me that the "girl friend" was actually "the other woman" in a triangle that had put this man in jail! Such situations point up the necessity for prayer for God's guidance and protection.

Don't be a "snitch" (informer). The pastor who goes to jail will in the course of time learn of things going on in the cell blocks that would be helpful to the guards or staff if they knew them. Yet, it could be that he has been permitted to learn these things as a way of testing him to see if he can be relied upon to keep a confidence. There are exceptions to this, of course, such as an indication one plans to commit suicide, or some activity that would endanger the lives of a number of inmates, or staff. It is well to know that the health and safety of inmates who turn informers is much in question, and a pastor will do well to keep his eyes and ears open and his mouth shut.

Don't forget the women.

> Women in prisons and jails are often isolated from the mainstream of institutional life and are left with nothing to do and no real opportunity for rehabilitation. What is often overlooked is that female inmates may be mothers and even wage earners for their families. One estimate said that on any given day there are 21,000 children of imprisoned mothers. When the mother is arrested, the children may be removed from their home and school and not allowed to see their parent. Both mother and children suffer anxiety because of this unnatural separation.[15]

Ethical considerations make it difficult for the preacher to minister to the female prisoners, but it is not impossible. Visits may be arranged to be carried on in full view of the matron overseeing their quarters, and yet still enable some counseling. I asked one matron if any of her charges wanted to see the chaplain, and a young woman in her early twenties came out, and seating was arranged right there in the room where the matron's desk was.

I asked, "What can I do for you?"

She replied, "I'm all mixed up, and don't know what to do."

"I don't know what I'd do if I were in your shoes, either," I said, "But there is One who has promised to guide us if we will trust Him. Look at this."

She read Proverbs 3:5-6 out loud, and then read it again silently. "That's what I need!" she exclaimed. "How do I go about it?"

At this point, a counselor came into the office and asked to see another of the inmates, and there was a lot of traffic as people went back and forth. Yet the young woman read passage after passage of Scripture in spite of all the distractions, ending with Christ's invitation in Matthew 11: 28-30 for all those who are heavy-laden to come to Him. Right there in full view of the matron and the counselor who was just leaving, inmate and pastor joined hands as she prayed, asking Jesus to come into her heart.

In a recent letter, she wrote, "It took your visits, Leah and Betty's visits, and some praying for me to get some sense into me—and I know now that truly the Lord watches over all of you. You reached me when I was down and out, and through your prayers and mine, I finally realized I needed to become the Lord's. . . . If it wasn't for Him, I could've been dead by now. . . . Your prayers for me helped me to turn my life around—for the better. I was a Lost Sheep—but you helped me find my way."16

Don't let disappointment throw you.

> The one who is called to minister to prisoners needs an *infinite capacity for disappointment.* Often he will fail to measure up to the needs of the moment. Perhaps because of tiredness or preoccupation with something else, he will not heed or adequately respond to an inmate seeking his help. Satan will use guilt feelings about such failures to discourage and destroy. Let every worker remember that God is not bound by our inadequacies and that He wastes nothing, not even our mistakes and failures, but weaves

them into His pattern for human history, even bringing good from our evil.[17]

When the disappointments come, the deflated servant of the Lord will do well to remember that it is God who gives the increase. He can fellowship with Elijah (1 Kings 19:10,14), who felt that he was the only real servant of God left in Israel; with Jeremiah, who would have just as soon had a house by the side of the road to minister to only those who *wanted* help (Jer. 9:1-8); and with the apostle Paul, who was forsaken by Demas (2 Tim. 4:10) and who had to face his first court hearing all alone (2 Tim. 4:16). And, he can accept God's invitation to unload it all on Him, being assured that He will lift up his servants (Ps. 55:22; 1 Pet. 5:7).

Recapitulation

The pastor who goes to jail will do well to check his motivation: is it selfish, or out of love for Christ and persons He died for? Are you called to this type of ministry, and will you obey that call?

You will also want to make the necessary preparation, both spiritually through prayer, Bible study, and meditation; and administratively through learning the ropes and people, and getting together the needed materials.

And, you will want to be familiar with do's and don'ts, some of which will be peculiar to the institution in which you work. Some you will learn by experience. As you go to this field, moved by the Spirit, you can anticipate God doing great things for His glory through your service there.

Arthur (not his real name) had been sentenced, and it was a tough one: twelve to twenty years. Having read this in the paper, I went to the cell block where he was, and found him seated at a table with three other inmates; a hand in a card game was ending.

"Saw your name in the paper."

"Yeah."

"How do you feel about it?"

"It's about what I thought they'd do to me."

"Arthur, the Lord is going to use you where you are going," I said, and then recounted to him how Joseph had been hated by his brothers, sold into slavery, sent to prison because his owner's wife lied about him, was forgotten by the chief butler of Pharaoh's court, but then ended up being prime minister of Egypt and the means of salvation to those very brothers who had sold him into slavery. Arthur read Genesis 45:4-8, in which Joseph pointed out that God had used his brothers to send him on ahead to Egypt to preserve their lives. "And He'll use you, too" I said.

"He's already using him," chimed in one of the other men. "I noticed when Arthur came on this block that he didn't use the same language most of the other guys use, and that he was reading his Bible every day, so I started to read it, too."

"That's great," I said, "Are you getting anything out of it?"

"Yeah, I'm learning a few things," he said, and then asked some questions about some things in the Book of Revelation.

"I'm glad to see you're picking up things like that," I responded. "But the Bible is a spiritual book, and it takes a spiritual experience in order to really understand it. Have you been born again?"

"I've been trying to be," he came back.

"Whoever heard of a baby trying to be born? Here, take a look at these verses." He took the New Testament from me, opened to John 3, and read the first eight verses. After a few words of explanation about the difference between the natural birth and the spiritual birth, I asked him, "Do you know why you have to be born again?"

"No, not really," he replied.

"Then look at these verses." This time the New Testament was open to Romans 3. But before he could begin reading, one of the men across the table said, "Read it out loud!"

"Yeah, read it out loud!" the fourth joined in.

And one man's changed life was the main factor in three more men coming to saving knowledge of the Lord Jesus Christ. There are plenty of rewards for the pastor who will take the time to go to jail.

Notes

1. *Prison People: A Guide for Prison Fellowship Volunteers.* (Washington: Prison Fellowship, 1981), page 43.

2. Frank Constantino, *Crime Fighter.* (Dallas: Acclaimed Books, (1981), page 27.

3. Ibid., p. 28.

4. *Prison People,* p. 43.

5. Duane Pederson, *How to Establish a Jail and Prison Ministry.* (Nashville: Thomas Nelson Publishers, 1979), pp. 77-78.

6. *Prison People,* p. 44.

7. *Prison People,* p. 43.

8. Pederson, p. 82.

9. Ibid., p. 79.

10. *Prison People,* p. 45.

11. Pederson, p. 83.

12. Pederson, pp. 80-81.

13. Ibid.

14. Constantino, p. 72.

15. Pederson, p. 69.

16. Personal letter to author.

17. Dale K. Pace, *A Christian's Guide to Effective Jail and Prison Ministries.* (Old Tappan, N.J., Fleming H. Revell Co., 1976), pp. 164-165.

4
What About
My Church?

The needs in the local jail are great with challenge and opportunity. The pastor needs to go to jail, and there is plenty in there for him to do. In fact, there is more than he can ever accomplish by himself. Moses had led the children of Israel out of captivity and slavery, and was headed toward the Promised Land, but he had a few things to learn. Jethro, his father-in-law, met him in the wilderness where he was camped, bringing Moses' wife and two sons.

The next day, Jethro observed that Moses spent the entire day listening to the complaints of the people and trying to help solve them. Later, Jethro got Moses to one side and told him, "What you are doing is not good. You and these people who come to you will only wear yourselves out. The work is too heavy for you; you cannot handle it alone" (Ex. 18:17-18, NIV). Then Jethro suggested a method to Moses that would spread the work and get others involved as well. It took a big load off Moses. More will get done in the jail if the pastor involves his church in the ministry there.

The tremendous fact of prison ministry is that it is an opportunity near at hand. Every community has at least a jail. Many others have correctional institutions, such as halfway houses, detention centers, and prisons. A church that is interested in prisoners doesn't have far to look.

It is this nearness that is also part of the shameful neglect by churches for prison ministries. Between 1,500 and 2,000 jails have no religious service for inmates. Many of these are small and medium-sized, but a few have several hundred inmates. Many detention centers, work farms, and other institutions also lack a consistent Christian witness. Too many churches are unaware of this need, or, regrettably, have turned aside from it. Yet every church can do *something* for prisoners.[1]

Many churches have trouble with farsightedness. They can become very active in drumming up support for foreign missions and for home missions in areas far from home, but are not involved to any great degree in the community needs around them. King Solomon wrote that "Where there is no vision, the people perish" (Prov. 29:-18). Churches need to have their bifocals on, lest they stumble over opportunities that are right under their noses.

Perhaps one of the things that make far-off foreign and home missions attractive is that, aside from giving some money and maybe writing some letters and praying, there is no real involvement. But church members need to be involved! There is more to the church than just having one's name on the roll and attending Sunday School and worship. It can be shown statistically that it is the uninvolved church member who falls easy prey to the cults and fringe organizations; it is the uninvolved church member who frequently is involved in friction and factions which create stress in the church. So the pastor who goes to jail needs help, and that help can best come from his own congregation. He already knows the people and where there are some who, while not really involved in the church, can be put to work in the outreach at the local jail.

Plan the Work

Size It Up.

If there is a local ministerial association, contact them to see what programs may already be in progress. Decide if there are known needs that are not being met. If there are more institutions than just the local jail, these should be included in a survey. Where possible, the warden, sheriff, jailer, or responsible person should be interviewed, and their suggestions solicited. Fellow pastors and church members may also be sources of information on what is being done and what needs to be done.

With this information gathered and interpreted, the next step is to determine what programs are needed, what resources are available, and which programs can be attempted with those resources. "For which of you, intending to build a tower, sitteth not down first, and counteth the cost, whether he have sufficient to finish it?" (Luke 14:28). The needs are so great, and the opportunities to minister to those needs so many, that there is a real danger of too many programs being attempted. Just one outreach program behind the bars well done can accomplish much more than many sloppily done or begun and later dropped. The survey and its analysis should be thorough and complete.

Pray

There are times when it seems this word is overworked, but its practice never is! "Pray ye therefore the Lord of the harvest, that he will send forth labourers into his harvest" (Matt. 9:38). Pray that the church will get a vision of what God wants to and can do through them as they become involved in serving in the local jail. Pray that a burden will come to members for the souls of those behind bars. Pray that God will definitely call men and women to work with the pastor in the jail.

Someone has said that men should pray as though the success of their efforts depends entirely upon God, and then work as though that success depended on themselves. In every work for the Lord, prayer is essential. It prepares and strengthens the worker. It opens doors and hearts, and puts words and actions in the mouths and hands and feet of the Lord's servants. Has He not said, "Call unto me, and I will answer thee, and shew thee great and mighty things, which thou knowest not" (Jer. 33:3)?

Present the Challenge to the Church

The information about needs and opportunities to meet them should be shared with the congregation. Possibly the warden or sheriff or some other official could be invited to outline possibilities at a special meeting or banquet. A sermon or series of sermons could be brought emphasizing the biblical mandate for followers of Jesus to be involved in ministering to those behind bars. Booklets and pamphlets can be secured and enclosed with Sunday bulletins, church handouts, and the church newsletter, and placed on literature tables. Former inmates can be encouraged to share their testimonies in worship services and at men's and women's meetings. Films on jail and prison ministries are available and may be shown. It has been observed that the people of God will respond favorably when they are well informed of needs and then challenged to meet them.

The people should be encouraged to pray for God to

lead, motivate, and to provide the workers and resources. Jesus said, "Again I say unto you, That if two of you shall agree on earth as touching any thing that they shall ask, it shall be done for them of my Father which is in heaven" (Matt. 18:19).

One chaplain says, "We need to put feet to our prayers by communicating clearly . . . what volunteer needs there are. . . . Plan job descriptions for each volunteer position to support the programmed ministry. It's much easier to enlist volunteers for tasks that are clearly outlined and not open-ended in their intended results. Insure that the tasks are necessary, not just 'busywork.' "2 He suggests providing printed commitment cards which would present the various options for a jail ministry program.

Secure Church Approval

While some members may see no need for a jail ministry and will not become involved in it, they are not likely to oppose it if they have been fully informed and the body has taken official action. The recommendation for church adoption of a jail ministry can come from the pastor himself, but likely would be better received if it came from the deacons, stewards, or elders, or from the organizations in the church through which men and women promote and support missions. When the church has acted, they are much more likely to be involved in *their* program than they are *the pastor's* program. Endorsement by the congregation will also provide a much better atmosphere for the enlistment and training of the workers needed, and open doors for future spots in the church budget to provide for literature and supplies.

Like just about any other form of outreach, a jail ministry has some expenses involved. Bibles, New Testaments, Bible study booklets, tracts, books, tapes and cassette players, stationery, and other supplies will be needed. An educated guess should be made and an allocation from the budget secured where possible. If financial matters are tight, church approval should be sought to seek individual contributions for needed materials. Inclusion in the budget in the future just the same as other programs of the church should be a goal.

Organize for Ministry in the Jail

If there is a church missions committee, it is the local route for administration of this church-approved outreach. If it is a large committee, a subcommittee could be formed; if a small committee, then one person should be chosen to help integrate the jail ministry into the mission outreach of the church. If there is no missions committee, then the challenge of the jail ministry might be the catalyst to bring one into being. Short of that, the missions organizations of the church for men and women should assume responsibility for oversight, promotion, and provision for the jail ministry of the church. Or, the church may wish to authorize a special committee of those who have expressed interest in this outreach to oversee it and report directly to them.

However the church chooses—organization, committee, or individual—regular reports should be rendered on progress, setbacks, victories, defeats, and needs, along with recommendations for any needed church action.

The pastor should enlist the workers personally, as they will be the ones who will reinforce his personal ministry in the jail. As he learns about the inmates and their needs, he can visualize some members of the church whom he feels could fit right in. If he has served long as pastor, he knows the idiosyncrasies and quirks some members may have which might either help or hinder their serving effectively behind the walls. From among those who have volunteered, he can, under the leadership of the Holy Spirit, choose men and women through whom God can minister in the jail. Before making contact with them, it might be well that he share their names with the church nominating committee. After they have agreed to serve, they should be elected by the church just as are workers in other church programs. Having church backing in a difficult assignment will be a source of comfort and assurance to them.

Train the Workers

"The promised training of volunteers is a great incentive to recruitment. Often people are reluctant to volunteer for strange new jobs for fear of not knowing how to do them. Training the volunteers is essential to an effective program."[3]

Arrange for some orientation to the institution as a first step in developing interest and (as often happens) in "weeding out" those persons who feel uncomfortable with this type of ministry.

Within the church, hold orientation sessions with the core of potential volunteers, perhaps seeing a film on prisons, reading materials on prison work, and discussing principles of effective prison volunteerism. Use this as a time to explore personal motivations, and to study the biblical basis of your ministry. Make sure every volunteer clearly understands what your ministry is and what its limitations are.[4]

Worker training should include the principles, qualifications, and do's and don'ts of chapter 3. It should include discussion of the rules and procedures of the institution, instructions on how to present the gospel and to lead inmates to a decision for Christ, and directions for answering the usual objections. Role playing can be a very effective means of getting these truths across. In addition to classes, training should also include some "required reading" on the criminal justice system (so workers can be familiar with some of the terms that will come up in conversations with inmates) and on jail ministry. (See bibliography.)

Some persons who may be apprehensive about working inside the jail may still be interested in prison outreach, and can serve in other capacities, such as record keeping, inmate correspondence, Bible course grader, and releasee follow-up. They will need to be in on the "inside training" so that they will be familiar with what goes on, and will also need instruction in their own responsibilities.

Work the Plan

"It is important that volunteer programs be conducted properly. Bad volunteer experiences cannot only hurt people (volunteer, offender, or both), but can also create a very bad attitude in the institution toward volunteer programs and seriously damage a program's reputation in the community. These things can limit a ministry to prisoners. . . . Any volunteer program should be implemented slowly and carefully, using initially only the cream of the crop in terms of both volunteers and offenders. Then after the bugs have been worked out of the program, it can be expanded."[5]

Things that church members can do inside the jail are determined by security considerations, availability of facilities, total population, degree of cooperation by the institutional staff, secular programs going on inside the jail, and time the volunteer can give, among others. Among the possibilities for participation and service are:

Worship Services

Church volunteers can give their personal testimony; sing solos or participate in ensembles or choirs; play instruments; lead in prayer; read Scripture; counsel those making decisions; provide fellowship. The latter is particularly important to both new and old Christians. It is surprising sometimes what just "being there" can mean to folks who have little or no relationships with believers behind the bars.

Showing Christian Films.

Through films, church members can witness inside the jail and relieve the pastor of some responsibilities. If the facilities are such that movies can be shown, a schedule for monthly or even weekly showings could be arranged. The purpose is not to entertain but to instruct and inspire. There are many productions which have an excellent plot and, at the same time, present the gospel. Films shown should be of the kind that call for a decision for Christ, and church members presenting them should be prepared to extend an invitation for public commitment and to counsel with inmates who make decisions. Names should be given to the pastor for follow-up.

In many institutions inmates have access to television sets in their cells or on the blocks. With nothing to do, they tire of soap operas, game shows, situations comedies, and the like, and welcome something different. Some prisons and jails have inmate television sets tied to a videocassette system, and show movies to inmates in this fashion. More and more Christian films are also being put on tape, and this avenue of presenting the truth should be explored.

Cassette Tape Ministry

This was suggested in chapter 3, but there is much more to this than a pastor can administer. Church members can keep records, audit tapes to be heard by inmates, keep players in repair and playing heads clean, see that tapes are evenly distributed among inmates, and attend to the multitude of minor irritations that arise. Not only are Bible and preaching tapes available, but also a large number of instructional tapes which help prepare for high school equivalency tests, jobs, and careers. How much a tape ministry can accomplish is limited only by the number of volunteers, available facilities, and security considerations inside the institution.

Special Musical Programs

Music can be offered by church members at regular chapel services or on special occasions, within the bounds of jail policies and security considerations. Inmates who would never attend a worship service for the preaching will come for the music, and special all-music presentations tend to draw a large participation. Such programs should include testimonies by members and a presentation of the gospel with an invitation to accept Christ. Again, names should be shared with the pastor.

At some jails there are no facilities for chapel services, no dayrooms or other places where programs can be offered. With administration concurrence, however, volunteers may go from one group of cells to another with the gospel in song. Prisoners should be invited to join in singing old familiar hymns and tunes.

Teach Bible Classes

Inside the jail, members can teach to small groups of men or women. Since the turnover in the local lockup tends to be high, class material must necessarily be of the kind that calls for short duration, a month at most, for a unit. If possible, separate classes should be held for "seekers" and for believers, so that on the one hand the Word may be presented, and on the other those who know the Lord may be helped in their spiritual growth. An early morning Sunday School class or two are also possibilities. Volunteers involved in Bible classes should secure names, birthdays, and other pertinent information. Absentees and prospects can be cultivated in the same way as a class in the church, and the class itself be included in the records of the Bible-teaching program of the church. Decisions made in the classes should be shared with the pastor for follow-up.

Bible correspondence courses attract some inmates who will not attend regularly scheduled classes. Several organizations offer these, and provide grading and counsel for inmates. Church members may offer advice, and the courses may be administered through the church. Members may hand out written invitations for inmates to sign up for courses, and may serve as graders and record keepers. If there are enough volunteers, handling the course through the local church can provide that personal touch prisoners need, and affords the opportunity for a continuing ministry when they are transferred to other institutions.

Teach Work Skills

Many inmates have dropped out of school early and have no trade or profession. A stint in jail helps them to realize the need for this, and, with plenty of time on their hands, many will attend the classes and study the materials. As the instructor shares the secrets and techniques of such things as welding and upholstering, he can also share his own personal testimony and point his class members to the One who gives purpose to life.

Pray with Inmates

Prayer with inmates is one important ministry that church members can conduct. Many prisoners are "afraid" of pastors and professional prople and will not open up to them. But as church members conduct various ministries in the jail and come to be known, confidence in them will develop, and those behind the bars will share burdens with them. Nearly every inmate carries a burden of guilt, real or imagined, and has a need for someone to show enough concern for them to pray with them. Their needs are especially acute at the crisis times mentioned earlier, and here is a place where the alert volunteer may really strengthen the ministry of the pastor who goes to jail. Again, names of those whom the volunteer feels need follow-up should be passed on to the pastor.

Visitation

Just plain visiting can provide a vital witness for Christ to inmates. In addition to spending time with them during scheduled activities, a volunteer can show real concern by going to the jail during visiting hours for personal one-to-one contacts. Such visits may develop into counseling sessions, and the inexperienced and untrained volunteer would do well to observe, "Now, that's getting out of my territory," or something like that. One should never be afraid or ashamed to say, "I don't know the answer to that," and if it is something that can have answers, offer to see what the answer is and share it later.

One approach to a visitation-counseling ministry is to have teams of volunteers who report to a volunteer coordinator. This person provides communication with the jail or prison administrators, answers questions from volunteers, and gets information from the institution. Volunteer teams should plan to meet together prior to visiting an institution and then again following the visit, so they can share problems, questions, and good experiences. Volunteers working in teams can encourage and support one another and are likely to be more effective than individual volunteers working alone.[6]

Visitors should do everything possible to encourage inmates to better themselves, not only by a personal relationship with the Lord Jesus, but also in education and training which may be available in the institution. Inmates should understand that, while church members may not approve of their behavior, they do approve of them, and should have the assurance that there is someone on the "outside" who is interested in them and pulling for them.

Small groups may be permitted by some jail administrators, and church members who have the gift of leadership in this area can find themselves involved in some fruitful experiences. Rapid inmate turnover tends to hinder this approach to ministry, as small group effectiveness depends upon continuity and participants becoming open to share with one another; nevertheless, some jail inmates are there on sentence and can provide stability to such an outreach. If jail authorities are willing to provide the information, small groups can be formed from willing prisoners who are on specified sentences.

Recreation

Most local jails have no facilities for recreation, and some which do have no organized program. If a survey reveals facilities available but no program; or, if inmates can be transported with proper security to a place where they can engage in such activities as basketball, volleyball, tennis, badminton, handball, or other such physical activities, then church members experienced in these sports may provide organization and leadership. Much of the violence inside jails comes about because of pent-up energies which have no means of release, and such a program will not only show concern, but also perhaps prevent personal injuries and even longer terms behind bars for inmates. Again, there will be opportunities for sharing faith in Christ in such settings. This is a much needed ministry.

Letter Writing

Another service volunteers from the church may perform is that of letter writing. As noted earlier, many inmates have reading problems, and it thus follows that they have writing difficulties. They want to communicate with family members and friends, and are frustrated because of their inability to do so. They may "dictate" a letter to the church member, or simply give an idea of the message they want to convey, and the helper can write it for them, then read it back to make sure there are no discrepancies before it is mailed. This is another way that real care and concern for inmates may be shown.

Correspondence with inmates is a ministry which may be performed by those who do not feel led to join in the efforts behind the walls, yet are concerned about and interested in prisoners.

It must be made crystal clear in letter writing that the

relationship is to be on a *spiritual* level. When letter writers talk about "love," it should be plain that it is *God's*
love. Writers should not leave themselves open to be
"used" by inmates, either while they are behind bars or
when they are released. It can be exciting and rewarding,
but also depressing and frustrating. One writer suggests:

1. Do not use a home address when you are corresponding
with prisoners—use a *post office box number,* or have your
letters channeled through your church or another ministry organization. This avoids problems.
2. When you are writing to prisoners to share Jesus, remember your mission. It is very easy to get personally
involved with someone at the other end of a pen. Prisoners
are lonely, and it is easy for them to "respond" to kindness
with the wrong reaction. If this happens, generally you
have a very short time to "nip it in the bud" and get them
back on the track. If your intentions are made clear from
the start, you will usually be able to avoid such situations.[7]

He adds other suggestions about encouraging the
recipients, about being positive in approach, not prying
about reasons for imprisonment, and says that whenever
a promise is made, it should be kept. The letter writer
should be careful to magnify Jesus, and any denominational issues that are raised should be played down, he also
says.

Who is going to harm you if you are eager to do good?
But even if you should suffer for what is right, you are
blessed. "Do not fear what they fear; do not be fright-
ened." But in your hearts set apart Christ as Lord. Always
be prepared to give an answer to everyone who asks you
to give the reason for the hope that you have. But do this
with gentleness and respect, keeping a clear conscience,
so that those who speak maliciously against your behavior

in Christ may be ashamed of their slander (1 Pet. 3:13-16, NIV).

It goes without saying that the underlying purpose in all church member service inside and outside the jail is to "give the reason for the hope" that they have in the Lord Jesus. They can share their personal testimonies as opportunities arise, and should take steps to create an atmosphere where they can share it. And every volunteer serving inside the walls should be equipped with good gospel tracts and booklets to reinforce their witness. God says, "So shall my word be that goeth forth out of my mouth: it shall not return unto me void, but it shall accomplish that which I please, and it shall prosper in the thing whereto I sent it" (Isa 55:11).

Caution Lights

Church members in jail ministry need to be reminded that there are some dangers involved in their service and that they should take steps to avoid and protect themselves from these hazards to which they voluntarily are exposing themselves. "Discretion is the better part of valor."

There is, of course, a certain amount of physical danger. One man, talking to an inmate in his cell, leaned closely to better hear what he was saying. He was wearing a tie, which the prisoner grabbed and proceeded to bang his head against the cell bars until others came and pulled him off.[8] That incident shows that attention must be given to dress. Women volunteers who participate in worship services and Bible studies in which male inmates are involved should dress conservatively and be cautious not to act in any way which inmates could misunderstand or misinterpret. Volunteers should never forget that some inmates are behind bars because they are violent, and avoid situations which could place them in danger.

The warning about emotional involvement in letter writing needs to be repeated with regard to all jail activities. Some prisoners can just be absolutely winsome when it suits their purposes, and more than one volunteer has been so taken in that they begin to wonder why such a wonderful person is in jail. Yes, it is difficult to carry out the Master's commandment to love everyone without becoming emotionally involved. When a volunteer realizes this is happening to him or her, it should be discussed with the pastor or another volunteer, and the relationship should be gotten into the proper focus or terminated. Continuation can result in harm to both inmate and volunteer, and possible compromise of the witness inside the walls.

There is one aspect of emotional involvement that needs to be highlighted: the danger of getting "conned." In fact, this can happen to volunteers even without their becoming entangled with an inmate. An experienced prison minister says, "Some prisoners attempt to manipulate unsuspecting volunteers, but . . . the majority of the prison population is sincere, seeking, and in need of ministry. . . . If prospective ministers (be they male or female) are not sufficiently able to deal with the ongoing manipulative techniques employed by certain types (only) of inmates, perhaps it would be better for all concerned if they continued being discipled (themselves) before embarking on any attempt to disciple."[9]

Institutional rules are constantly changing, and are subject to varied interpretations by different staff members, and by different shifts. There should be regular review of these rules and policies by volunteers, and the administration should be consulted frequently to see if there have been any unpublicized changes.

Evaluate

One of the keys to any effective church program is consistent evaluation. There should be periodic review of the jail ministry of the church by the missions committee or whatever group has been put in charge by the congregation. Goals and objectives should be determined, and criteria established. The prison work should be evaluated in the light of the overall goals and objects of the church, and any needed alterations discussed and brought to the body. With the objectivity such an arrangement provides, the pastor can serve much more effectively behind the bars.

There should be self-evaluation by the volunteers, too.

Periodically volunteers need to review their efforts with open minds, and to realize that there is a process of disillusionment that follows the challenging call to glorify God in the mission fields of this country's prisons. Bill Smith, Special Projects Administrator for Dade County, Florida, tells us that ". . . Volunteers should be aware of the 3-phase cycle that they themselves go through on their way to being "professionals" in the system: (1) enchantment, (2) disenchantment, and (3) growing through the disenchantment to a workable reality which allows the volunteer a productive portion in the life-transforming process.[10]

Review

There is simply no way that the pastor who goes to jail can do all that needs to be done by himself. He needs helpers, and those helpers can be found in the church where he serves. The church needs to have a vision of the ripe harvest field and needs to be involved in the work to be done there. A survey should be made to find out what, if anything, is presently being done by others in the jail, what additional programs, if any, are needed, and what resources are available. After prayer, the church should be informed and challenged, their approval and financial support secured, organization for administration carried out, and volunteers solicited, enlisted, and trained. With endorsement and cooperation of jail administrators secured, needed ministries should be carried on by members to support and strengthen the witness of the pastor. They should be evaluated, adjusted, or revised as other needs become apparent while some are met. The pastor who goes to jail with his church behind him through dedicated and trained volunteers can anticipate a harvest to bring glory to God.

The mechanics of starting a prison or jail ministry are not difficult. The difficulty comes with the initial awareness and with accepting a concern for prisoners as a biblical mandate and a ministry that is within the reach of almost any local church. In many communities, if the local churches do not take the initiative to establish and maintain a Christian witness in the jails and prisons, it will not happen at all. The church is not a refuge from the world; it is a training ground for people who will faithfully care and serve those in the world who are so much in need of the love and grace of Jesus Christ. In the prisons and jails of America are hundred of thousands of people who very much want to hear of that love and grace. I hope the reply of your heart is that of the prophet Isaiah: "Here am I; send me."[11]

Notes

1. Duane Pederson, *How to Establish a Jail and Prison Ministry.* (Nashville: Thomas Nelson Publishers, 1979), pp. 97-98.

2. Gerald R. Chancellor, "Establishing a Chaplaincy Program with a Corps of Volunteers in the County Detention Center," *AEIC Journal,* n.d.

3. Ibid.

4. Pederson, page 102.

5. Dale K. Pace, *A Christian's Guide to Effective Jail & Prison Ministries.* (Old Tappan, N.J.: Fleming H. Revell Co., 1976), pp. 154-155.

6. Pederson, ibid.

7. Frank Constantino, *Crime Fighter.* (Dallas: Acclaimed Books, 1981), p. 81.

8. Correctional Chaplaincy Course Notes, January 6, 1982.

9. Constantino, p. 78.

10. Ibid., p. 83.

11. Pederson, p. 103.

5
There's More?

One of the shortcomings of many jail ministries is that they are too much like the local church programs. Evangelical churches major on both making disciples, and baptizing them, and then, having told them, "Take a seat right over here," they forget them. There seems to be a mistaken assumption that new disciples for Christ will just grow by themselves, without any guidance or encouragement from those who have been so eager to sign them up and get them baptized. Far too often, the jail inmate who has made a decision for Christ is rejoiced over and then forgotten or ignored. Follow-up is of vital importance to the new child of God, to his influence on others behind bars with him, and to the effectiveness of the outreach in the jail.

Living for Christ while under confinement is difficult, and presents a real challenge. The person who makes a public commitment to Him can expect ridicule, harassment, and even persecution from his peers. What few belongings he has in his cell may turn up missing (no one knows what has happened to them!) or ruined. His Bible and other spiritual helps may be torn apart or an "accident" can happen by coffee or something worse being "spilled" on them. Attempts to read the Bible can result in the television being turned up to full volume, a loud discussion being moved to the cell, or other distractions. And, in crowded prison conditions where privacy is nonexistent, praying is next to impossible, and attempts at it will also meet with scorn and obstructions from fellow inmates.

Efforts to share the faith are met with such rejoinders as, "If you're so good, what are you doing in here?" It is not unusual for the new believer to be "set up" so that a surprise shakedown will turn up contraband among his things, thus getting him written up by the administration, with resultant blots on his record that could have bearing on his release. The list could go on and on. Perhaps more than in any other place, a follower of Jesus who is in jail needs help, especially if he has only recently made his decision.

> When an inmate has been reached for Christ, the role of the chaplain changes from that of evangelist to that of pastor. In order to develop wholesome maturity, the convert needs (1) spiritual knowledge, (2) a daily devotional life, (3) a Christian lifestyle, (4) fellowship with other believers, and (5) participation in service to Jesus Christ. Follow-up helps these needs to be met. Converted inmates who have become solid, mature Christians have been the object of much follow-up effort.[1]

In the last chapter, the multiplication of the efforts of the pastor who goes to jail through the enlistment and services of volunteers was emphasized. Some of the most valuable assistance that the preacher can have will come from those who have made commitments to Christ behind the bars, and have boldly and unashamedly shared their faith. Some prisoners will not listen or even talk to a minister—just think what doing that would do to their image in the eyes of their peers! But they do talk all the time to fellow inmates. Grounding in the faith and training are vital to the work.

As I walked onto the cell block one day, I was immediately accosted by one of the inmates who came from my right. "Hey, Rev, you in a big hurry? I'd like to talk to ya a minute. Come on in the cell." He proceeded to relate how he had been reviewing his life since he came into the jail. He said, "The other day I got to talking to Jack Worsham (not his real name), and he was tellin' me how his life had changed since he asked Jesus to come into his heart. I asked him what he meant, and he told me that when he first came in here, he did what I'm doing right now—carrying on a self-inventory, I guess. Said you'd come around and handed him some stuff to read and told him he'd find the answers in the Bible. He found one in another cell in here, and got to readin' it, and, even though it was hard to find 'em, he found some of the verses that were in the stuff you gave him. Said that the more he read, the more he wanted to read, and one night when just about everybody was asleep, he got on his knees by his bunk and prayed, and got saved. I think that's what I need!"

If Jack had not witnessed, there would never have been the opportunity to talk to this man! Jack shared his faith because he was growing in the Lord. What can the minister and volunteers from his church do to help spiritual growth?

The best place to look for advice on spiritual matters is in the Bible. The conversion of that archenemy of the growing, new church, Saul of Tarsus, is recorded in Acts 9:1-9. But unlike so many modern conversion stories, this one continues on down through verse 22. First, the Lord sent a reluctant Ananias to minister to him. The man who had been blind to the hand of God working through the followers of the Way, and who had been physically blind himself for three days, received his sight. He both saw and perceived things that were completely new to him! Though the Scripture does not here say so, no doubt Ananias explained to him that those who receive Jesus as Savior make that commitment public by being baptized; Saul had prayed, "Lord, what wilt thou have me to do?" (v. 6). So he was baptized. He had been without food and drink three days; now he "received meat" and was strengthened. It is quite likely that he was served spiritual food along with the meals he ate.

Then he was with the disciples in Damascus "certain days," meaning that these formerly apprehensive and suspicious believers extended to Saul the right hand of fellowship. That was very important to him then, and it is also to new believers today. With the strength from the food and the assurance from the fellowship, he immediately preached in the synagogues that Christ is the Son of God. The care and guidance of Saul's new brothers in Christ helped to speed him along the road to spiritual growth, and made him bold to witness for the Lord even in a hostile environment.

While They're Still There

Follow-up programs for inmates are subject to the same limitations as the rest of the jail ministry: administration cooperation, jail rules and procedures, facilities, and time the pastor and volunteers can allot. Within these restrictions several approaches are possible.

Individual Counsel

Where possible, this is desirable as soon as possible. Thus the pastor and the prisoner can go over the decision that has been made to determine if it was a first time

commitment, or renewal of vows, and work toward reso-
lution of questions the new convert may have. This gives
the minister the opportunity to show personal interest
and concern, and to personally encourage his "client" in
spiritual growth. The preacher can provide him with tools
that will help him in his walk: a Bible, if he has none; first
lesson for a Bible study, or invitation to participate in a
correspondence Bible study; daily devotional guide; tracts
and booklets giving an explanation of and the steps in
spiritual growth. He may want to share names of other
believers on the same block for fellowship purposes, and
give information about programs being conducted in the
jail to aid spiritual growth.

A Class for New Christians

This may be conducted if there are enough new con-
verts to warrant it. A class will enhance the pastor's jail
ministry if he is the teacher; however, a mature volunteer
may elicit more openness from the inmates. Such a class
should include topics like how to become a Christian,
what the Bible is and how to use it, witnessing, prayer,
how to know the will of God, and the cardinal doctrines
of the Christian faith that are held by all denominations.
The highly transient nature of jail populations will neces-
sitate that considerable study be given to the content of
such a class.

Bible Study

Learning God's Word is vital to the growth of the new
Christian.

A program for consistent Bible study should be offered so
as to allow the new convert to become rooted and grounded in the Word of God which is necessary nourishment for

the new believer according to 1 Peter 2:2 which says, "As newborn babes, desire (imperative) the sincere (pure) milk of the word, that ye may grow thereby." This kind of program may be offered on an individual self-study or class basis.[2]

Some inmates will not want to join a class, at least not right away. They should be urged to participate in a correspondence Bible course. Several are available at no cost to the inmate other than postage, and some will be counted upon successful completion as credits toward a Bible school or even college diploma. Most offer a certificate upon completion of certain groups of lessons. The author has seen such certificates proudly displayed on cell walls. Such courses are designed to start where the prisoner is, and to help him first of all to know the Lord (some press for decisions) and then to grow in knowledge of Him. The certificate system tends to motivate correspondents to continue in the course. Encouragement from the pastor and from volunteers, with commendation for certificates awarded, are also motivating factors. Where possible, local grading of correspondence courses, with encouragement and commendation, also shows love and concern for the inmate.

Some of the best learning situations are those in which there can be interaction with others, and prisoners should be encouraged to participate in Bible study classes. Within security and administration considerations, small classes, with no more than six or eight participants, are the most effective. They work through the small group principle that people are reluctant to speak up and get involved when groups are larger. Again, the transient nature of the populations in local jails requires that materials for classes have a short-duration curriculum.

Fellowship

The pastor and volunteers from the church should provide as many opportunities for Christian fellowship as possible. Always mindful of jail rules and procedures, and of security considerations, chapel worship services should include time for interaction of inmates with those who know the Lord. The right "climate" is important to optimum growth, and every effort should be made to generate that climate. A word of caution is necessary at this point: "fellowship" does not mean "familiarity." As noted previously, inmates are lonely, and innocent actions can be wrongly interpreted. Volunteers should be reminded to "abstain from all appearance of evil," and inmates should be warned that loss of privileges can result from too "warm" a response to fellowship.

Good Reading Material

The preacher working in the jail should see to it that new believers have plenty of good reading material to aid their growth in Christ. Much reading matter that circulates in jail is not fit for human eyes, and it must be remembered that the old nature is not immediately eradicated when one makes a decision for Christ. Books, pamphlets, periodicals, and tracts on spiritual growth should be given personally to those known to have made commitments to the Lord. Helpful articles in periodicals can be pointed out and recommended.

Graduate Equivalency Diploma

If there are no courses being offered at the jail, the minister working there should, through volunteers, seek to establish one. If one is in existence, he should encourage participation by the new convert. At times learning to read better has opened many spiritual doors for the inmates. They should be encouraged to take advantage of all opportunities presented for self-improvement.

Spiritual "Buddy"

To further aid in the spiritual growth of some prisoners, the pastor who goes to jail may want to arrange for a "spiritual buddy" from the outside, either a correspondent, or one who will visit in a one-to-one counseling program, or both. Many inmates have very low self-esteem, and to have visits and letters from someone who shows they really care can go a long way in helping them to know that they are important to God, too.

Tapes

Cassette tapes can also provide an avenue for helping spiritual growth of new believers. Just as the pastor may suggest good books, he may also point out certain tapes that are available on prayer, Bible study, witnessing, and other such "vitamins and minerals" of improving the walk with the Lord. These tapes should be included in the cassette ministry referred to in an earlier chapter.

It may seem to the reader that there is much duplication of what has already been prescribed for the entire jail ministry, and there is. But the things suggested above for new children of God are in addition to the regular chapel services, Christian films, and Bible classes. In other words, a pastor who goes to jail needs to see that those who have made decisions for Christ are taught to observe His commandments as He ordered.

When They Leave

Many inmates will go through several institutions during their time of incarceration. The inmate may be held in several jails while being tried upon a variety of charges once he has been apprehended. Then he may go to the receiving unit or diagnostic center of the state prison system before being sent to the unit where he will serve his time. Even then, he may be transferred to another unit (as his security classification changes, because of threats upon his life, for needed medical treatment, etc.). A good chaplain is concerned about the spiritual growth of his "son in the faith" through such meanderings.[4]

The local jail may send inmates to one of several institutions in the state system. The pastor who is concerned about the continued spiritual growth of those he has seen come to know the Lord will want to learn what spiritual programs there are available. Some are conducted by parachurch organizations such as Prison Fellowship; others are carried on by local churches or ministerial associations. If he knows a pastor in the area, he may wish to contact him, and suggest a personal visit and ask for names of contact persons in the institution's spiritual programs. Most such prisons have a chaplain, and he should be advised of the new inmate's arrival, also. It should be noted, however, that many state and federal prison chaplains are viewed by inmates as "professionals" who are more concerned about their jobs than they are inmates. The pastor should check (former inmates in the jail are good information sources) to find out what he can about the chaplain at the state prisons.[5]

Before the inmate leaves, he should be encouraged to write to the pastor and/or church volunteers who have ministered to him in the jail. If the church has a newsletter, it would be encouraging to him to receive it as a reminder of the church's interest in and concern for him. Volunteers who may have corresponded with him in the jail should be encouraged to continue writing to him.

Strange to say, many prisoners who have become Christians in jail are interested in the progress of the programs there, and are concerned about the spiritual welfare of some of their fellow inmates. They like to hear news about the work, and about the church. The pastor and volunteers should make every effort to keep in touch with inmates who have left the jail for other institutions, and encourage them to continue in the faith.

A much-neglected but very important ministry is that of continuing the follow-up with inmates who are released. Releasees are very nervous; they *know* they will be back unless they have really changed. "Many volunteers get caught up in the glamour of working with inmates in prison. But few still minister to these people in the crucial days after they reenter the community. Yet ex-inmates need help at this stage more than ever."[6] The prime objective of the pastor's follow-up efforts should be to get the person actively involved in a local church, and then entrust his future discipleship to the leadership of that church.[7] If the ministry of the pastor and volunteers has been effective, he may wish to unite with their church. This should be encouraged, but not pushed. However, once the ex-inmate has made a choice, watchful care should continue.

There are several things that can be done for the ex-inmate through the local church. As noted earlier in chapter 3, the pastor should lead the congregation to organize for jail ministry, and this should include follow-up. Those who do not work inside the walls may still be of invaluable assistance to a releasee by using their talents and professions to help him in his adjustments to society. It must be realized that he is coming out of a restricted environment, and that the adjustments are critical. It requires good judgment and wisdom to help him make it in the frightening, bewildering world he enters after being locked away from society, sometimes for several years.

One of the first problems he will run into will be housing. Many landlords do not want ex-prisoners for tenants, and good living quarters are often difficult to find, much less to pay for. A healthy resumption of family life may well depend upon this critical factor. The pastor, through the church organization that administers the jail work, can lead in provision of funds for that first deposit in the budget. Landlords in the community can be enlisted who will cooperate with the congregation in this effort. From a "crisis closet" can come some items essential to setting up housekeeping.

Equally critical is employment. Businessmen can be enlisted who will take a chance on the releasee by giving him the opportunity to earn his way.

> After imprisonment and release, obtaining employment is even more difficult than ever . . . often an ex-offender never had any solid employable skills. Depending upon the length of incarceration, the ex-felon may find upon release that his skill has dwindled from non-use, or perhaps become dated from advances in technology. This puts him in an emotional as well as financial dilemma. Sometimes in his mind he excuses a crime as a means of survival or "getting even" with society for not having a chance at the "better life."[8]

The promise of a job is often one of the requirements for parole; yet most employers are understandably reluctant to hire persons with records of law infractions. When approached with the needs of a former inmate, they may be reminded as Christians that Jesus has chosen to work through men even though they have fallen. There are also tax advantages to those who hire ex-offenders. The pastor who cares will do what he can to help those who have been reached for Christ through his ministry in the jail.

Imprisonment has so scarred some that they have lost their initiative and drive. The preacher should be patient and persistent. If a want ad seems promising, it can be pointed out. If transportation is needed, it can be offered by the pastor or a volunteer.

Another ministry is to help ex-prisoners find needed services. With regard to employment, for example, not only should the state employment facility be located, but also on hand should be information about state or federal job-training programs in the area, and the availability of union apprentice programs for ex-offenders.

Studies have revealed that four out of five of all prisoners have some history of alcohol or drug abuse; some who have found Christ behind bars will, when released, go back to these old ways. They should not be dropped, but efforts should be made to channel them into Alcoholics Anonymous and other community services which minister to these problems. And it goes without saying that pastors and volunteers involved in follow-up with discharged prisoners should be familiar with public assistance offices and other related services as well.

An ex-felon's reintroduction into the community is bound to be a time of extreme anxiety. You, as a volunteer, must be sensitive to this anxiety. Think about the inner feelings of a person entering into a new and often hostile environment with no one to encourage and uphold them. It's frightening! I believe the absence of needed support is a prime factor of recidivism. Without support and direction, the newly-released ex-convict is severely tempted to return to his former "friends" and associates. It is imperative that we in After Care ministry break the crime—prison—release—crime—prison cycle: the ex-felon must not be allowed to return to his former friends and pattern of life—the same things that sent him to prison in the first place.[9]

Recap

Living for Christ is not easy anywhere, especially not in jail or prison. An inmate's peers can make it really rough for him if he is sold out to the Lord, and he needs plenty of help. Yet too many pastors and other volunteers who work among prisoners tend to neglect these new babes in Christ once they have been won. There especially needs to be emphasis upon "teaching them to observe" once they have made that commitment. This should be done by the pastor while they are still in jail through counsel, classes, Bible study, good reading material, Christian fellowship, and a buddy where possible. When they leave for another institution, they should be encouraged to write, and believers in the area of the new home should be advised. When they are released on parole or complete their sentence, the pastor and church should take steps to help them integrate into society. A pastor who goes to jail with a loving church behind him, ministering to new believers in the institution, in other institutions, and "on the street" will be a tool in the Lord's hands to curb recidivism (repeats) and to show his love to those whom society has written off, but the Lord has not.

A former inmate at the Erie County (Pennsylvania) prison wrote (the spelling is just as he wrote it):[10]

First of all I want to no how you are done. I am done OK now. As longing the Lord Jesus Christ be within my heart, because he walk with me each and every day, and I am thankful that the Lord that I am here. I have been praising the Lord ever since, and working for Jesus, telling everybody the Good News, what thy has done for me at the Erie

County Prison. The Lord has used me to win two others to Christ; I know it is true that when you are thankful and praising God for everything that happens to me He have blessed me with joy and peace and love.

It is cold to be in the cell up here. I no my Lord because He is with me. And I hope that you can find it in your heart to praising for me, why I am up here in this prison. I am praising that the will make a way for me to get in a Christian program why I am here, and if I happens moves from where I am I will conting to write to you.

Because a pastor and volunteers went to jail, a man was won to Christ; because of follow-up through counsel and literature, he became a soul-winner, and the Lord is still following up on him.

Notes

1. Dale K. Pace, *A Christian's Guide to Effective Jail and Prison Ministries.* (Old Tappan, N.J.: Fleming H. Revell Co., 1976), p. 161.

2. Gerald R. Chancellor, "Follow Up Inside the Institution," *AEIC Journal,* July, 1981, p. 11.

3. Ibid., p. 12.

4. Pace, p. 162.

5. Ibid., p. 164.

6. *Prison People.* Washington: Prison Fellowship, 1981, p. 46.

7. Pace.

8. Frank Constantino, *Crime Fighter.* (Dallas: Acclaimed Books, 1981), p. 89.

9. Ibid., pp. 91-92.

10. Personal letter to author.

6
Others Are Involved, Too!

There can be no doubt that the pastor who goes to jail can be effective in ministering there for the Lord Jesus Christ. The needs are tremendous, and opportunities for service are limited only by the resources available in finances, facilities, and personnel. But the inmate is not the only one who is affected by his incarceration, and his being behind bars creates a whole further set of needs which provide further open doors to service for the minister and his church.

> Several hundred thousand families are directly affected every year by having one of their loved ones in a prison or jail. This is a traumatic experience that can either shatter a family or, with love and attention from caring people, bring the family together to be a source of strength to the one in prison.[1]

"Religion that God our Father accepts as pure and faultless is this: to look after orphans and widows in their distress and to keep oneself from being polluted by the world" (Jas. 1:27, NIV). Wives and children of prisoners are not exactly widows and orphans, but they might as well be in many cases. Husbands in jail are not able to support them, so many exist on welfare or in poverty. The Book of James has something to say about those who see brothers or sisters naked and destitute of daily food, express concern for them, and yet do nothing to relieve their distress (Jas. 2:14-17).

> The family of the offender needs immediate help. There will be deep hurt and feelings of inadequacy. Since the prisoner must usually depend upon his family for help, the family in turn may need direct assistance. . . . This is a time of crisis and a time of openness to those who would assist.
>
> Few families of prisoners receive enough attention from the churches. Most of these families are broken, torn by strife and tension, generally disrupted, and filled with a great amount of anxiety. Many families experience extreme financial problems, in part because there is little knowledge of budgeting income. Others often cannot help themselves because, like the prisoner, the wives and children lack employable skills.
>
> Medical problems, bills, housing problems, and children difficult to control are common. Legal problems, including pending divorce actions, are to be expected.[3]

Pastors, churches, and individual Christians thus have many opportunities to show practical love and care for families in this situation. Just being there can be very important. Family members will be greatly encouraged in knowing that there are some people who are concerned about them and who are willing to help.

By far, the greatest percentage of inmates is men, and a very large proportion of them are married. Especially in jail, they are concerned about their families, as many of them are there for the first time, and in a state of shock and confusion. As the average age of prisoners in jail is under twenty-six, that means if there are children, they will be very young, and there is concern for them, too.

A study of prisoners and their families at the Illinois State

Penitentiary revealed that in most writings of prisoners (letters, prison newspapers and magazines), themes of "deep concern for the well-being of their families, despair at the separation, and resentment toward the justice system and society for imposing this forced separation" occur again and again. "I haven't heard from my wife" or "My husband hasn't written in a month" are typical and frequent comments from both sides of the prison walls.[3]

The pastor who goes to jail will, by ministering either himself or through church volunteers to families of those behind bars, reinforce and strengthen his witness there, while demonstrating that "God is no respecter of persons" and that all for whom Christ died are worthy in His sight.

> The divorce rate of men in prison is very high, but I'm inclined to believe that most family break-ups occur at the county jail level while the husband or wife is awaiting trial. "Dear Johns" come in the mail every day. Those in jail have the constant fear of losing their family added to all the other traumatic pressures. Ministry to families is among the most neglected areas of jail or prison ministries.[4]

Further insight into problems faced by inmate families may be gained from what one wife said in a talk on the subject, "How Prisoners' Wives React to the Incarceration of A Husband":

> As an inmate's wife, I found life very difficult. I discovered how cruel people can be—people that would not have been cruel when my husband was home. Men talk down to a woman who doesn't have a husband to back her up. . . . It's amazing how quickly men move in on a woman when they find out that her husband has been sent to prison (not necessarily sexually, although there is some of

that). They move in to pick the carcass of a broken home or family—to make a quick cash deal on a car if a woman needs a lawyer or money, or a possible house repossession if she can't keep up the payments. Many of our friends stopped coming by—they were afraid that I would ask for five dollars for food.

People were cruel to my children. It's hard to imagine adults picking on and heckling children because their father is a "jailbird." I had a difficult time dealing with that . . .

Women whose husbands are in prison generally have a very low self-image. They lose their self-respect. I felt as though I were useless, an outcast, stamped with a stigma of that prison sentence. There is a certain kind of paranoia attached to this kind of life. I really had the feeling that everybody knew what my situation was and where my husband was. This sense of low esteem was only accented by my visits to the county jail and to the prison.[5]

Not only wives and children, but also parents of inmates are affected by their being in jail. As they think about the incarceration of their son or daughter, one thing usually keeps coming back to them: "What did we do wrong? Where did we fail? What could we have done that we didn't do?" A pastor can perform an invaluable service in helping them to realize that each person is accountable for his own actions, and that in helping parents, he also helps inmates.

Parents may also be angry at God: "Why did He let this happen?" They will need pastoral support in working through this, and they will need the pastor's support as their offspring goes through the judicial processes to final disposition of the case. Pastors and churches, which are very solicitous when illness strikes or death comes, for the most part, do not seem to want to be involved when this kind of tragedy occurs, yet it is a time when concern and support can meet real needs and are deeply appreciated.

Though the families of prisoners need support from the Christian fellowship in a church, in reality it is often difficult or impossible to enlist them. The pastor and church volunteers can go to them as friendly visitors. "What the family needs is acceptance, not treatment as outcasts. This does not mean that one condones any criminal act, but that one sees all persons as human beings for whom Christ died—humans in need. The importance of simply having a friend can never be overstressed."[6] What can pastors and volunteers do to help?

There is no way to determine the value and strength of someone who will *listen.* The inmate will talk about his family when he senses that his hearers are paying attention and are concerned and interested. He will share his insecurities and frustrations, along with his love and dreams. Many times it will develop that his family's needs are what drove him to do the things that caused him to end up behind bars. The unsympathetic, impersonal legal system tends to harden him, as nothing he says seems to move those who administer the laws. The sympathetic listener will give him an opportunity to vent his anger and bitterness, and thus have a more objective view of himself. It is not necessary to agree with what he says, but just to have open ears and reflect interest and concern. "Bear ye one another's burdens, and so fulfil the law of Christ" (Gal. 6:2). As the prisoner senses that the pastor or volunteer really cares, through him doors will be opened to bring Christ to a hurting family.

Steps should be taken for a *visit* with the family. If, from conversations with the inmate, it appears that family relationships are good, it would be helpful if the inmate made the initial contact, suggesting that the pastor or some church members would be willing to call if it is so desired. A new believer behind bars might use this approach to share his own testimony of his experience with Christ, and give an avenue for sharing the faith, as well as providing some needed help. This way family members are introduced to the minister and his workers through someone they know. Wives of men behind bars tend to be suspicious of anyone who wants to talk to them, and the visit will be much more relaxed when it is suggested by the husband himself. Even then, the best approach is to visit only when invited by the family member. Since the time of preachers and church members is usually scarce, this will screen out many, and make possible productive visits with those who want someone to call on them. Here are some pointers for those who visit:

Preparation is important. Prayer will strengthen and reassure the visitor, and will open doors and hearts. Specific areas of concern to the inmate can be brought before the Lord prior to the contact. A marked New Testament, which can be used in witnessing and left in the home, should be included, along with tracts and booklets which might speak to needs apparent in discussions with the prisoner. When possible, visits should be made by teams of two, with one taking the initiative and the other praying. Visits by pastors, while they tend to create some nervousness, are especially appreciated, since there is sometimes the feeling that ministers visit very little, and that only to "worthy" people who might benefit the church in some way.

Visitors should be positive! The convicts' families are living in a negative world of gloom and frustration, and need positive affirmation. Any way that this may be done without being hypocritical will help bring rays of sunshine into an otherwise gloomy existence. It will require some study to keep from having negative reactions to some situations that are faced, but it can be done. The apostle Paul furnishes an example:

> Now I want you to know, brothers, that what has happened to me has really served to advance the gospel. As a result, it has become clear through the whole palace guard and to everyone else that I am in chains for Christ. Because of my chains, most of the brothers in the Lord have been encouraged to speak the word of God more courageously and fearlessly (Phil. 1:12-14, NIV).

He could have spent his time of imprisonment saying, "If only . . .," but Paul was positive about it, seeing the hand of God in all that was happening to him. The visitor who would be helpful should try to see the positive side of everything and help inmate families to do likewise.

Those who want to be of real help should be a friend, not a condescending outsider. Too many believers have a "Pharisee complex" which, if not kept in check, can cause them to look down on those who by their standards have not been as fortunate in life as they. Like inmates themselves, family members learn quickly to spot phonies, and have considerable contempt for them; in fact, it is not unheard of for them to con and use some who do the right things with the wrong attitudes. A friend is one who loves "in spite of" rather than "because of," and the worker who desires to be a tool in the hands of the Lord will remind himself that "there, but for the grace of God, go I." "A man that hath friends must shew himself friendly: and there is a friend that sticketh closer than a brother" (Prov. 18:24), especially when everything seems to be going wrong and nothing seems to work.

One recurrent theme in ministry to prisoners and their families is to listen! When someone from the household is in jail, frequently everyone else is tried, convicted, and sentenced, so to speak. Relatives and friends do not want to "get involved," afraid they may have to give up time to testify in court or at some hearing, or might have to come up with some cash to help pay rent or a car installment, or buy groceries, or help hire a lawyer. All this does is add to the anxieties and frustrations of those with loved ones behind the bars, and there is frequently no one to "unload" on. "My dear brothers, take note of this: Everyone should be quick to listen, slow to speak and slow to become angry" (Jas. 1:19, NIV). There is "a time to keep silence, and a time to speak" (Eccl. 3:7). Giving family members an avenue to ventilate to someone who is interested but unbiased can be a real service.

Pastors and workers who visit inmate family members should avoid arguments. No doubt many things in your conversation could provide fuel for disagreement. The argument could be won, and the privilege of being a friend and helper lost. A disarming approach would be, "While I don't agree with that, it doesn't mean we have to be disagreeable." Better still, the subject could be adroitly changed when a matter that could produce conflict arises. The purpose of the contact is to be of help, not to prove how adept one is in the Scriptures, social customs, or law interpretation. This outreach is to win friends for Christ, not arguments.

Discreetly and tactfully seek involvement in the church. In the warmth of Christian fellowship, hearts will be prepared to listen to the message of salvation by faith through Christ. Those who have heard about Christian love will have the opportunity to experience it. Seeds will be planted that can be cultivated with the goal of ultimate commitment to Christ. If transportation is a problem, it should be offered. Care is advised that actions taken not be interpreted as pressure of any kind to build numbers, but rather that there is genuine interest and concern.

Through visits, telephone calls, and other contacts, ministers and volunteers can help the family keep in touch. "It is important for the family to maintain some contact with the prisoner. The attitude of the family toward the inmate and toward imprisonment can have a beneficial or disastrous effect upon his progress while the offender is in prison."[7] A supportive family can frequently hasten parole, and help a releasee "go straight" once he is "on the street." Frequent exchanges of letters should be encouraged. The author has been on the cell block when mail call came, and noted the elation of some who heard from home, and the dejection of others who came away empty-handed.

Jail and prison visitation can be a real hassle, but the family should be encouraged to go every time possible. Sometimes difficulties and differences arise which cannot be adequately expressed or resolved through correspondence, and a face-to-face meeting can mean so much to both visited and visitor. Rules and times for personal visits vary widely from institution to institution, so workers with inmate families should familiarize themselves with their local situations and be ready to share information with inmates and family members. "Contact" visits, more private than those over a phone looking through glass, are needed from time to time, and may be easier by a recommendation from a pastor or volunteer who is respected by the staff.

Transportation can be provided. With the loss of a breadwinner often goes loss of the family car with no funds to pay for it, keep it in repair, and buy gas. Prisoner families need ways to get to the jail, to the doctor, to welfare offices, supermarket, drug store, and schools.

While it could be easy to fall into providing free taxi service, yet this can be a way of showing compassion, concern, and interest. Care should be taken to see that responsibility for providing transportation is spread over several volunteers, so that it becomes a burden to no one, and that no one gets "conned" into providing nonessential joyrides.

Preachers and volunteers should know the community resources for help.

> Many families do not know how to seek help available in the community. Referral services can be effective. Since financial and other limitations often prevent from obtaining dental, medical, and legal assistance needed, a needed service may be in helping locate organizations such as the Legal Aid Society, community health clinics, counseling agencies, or welfare agencies.[8]

The current availability to job training programs and daycare centers for mothers who would like to learn a skill and be self-supporting should be a part of the information kept up-to-date for those who seek to help families of inmates.

The pastor who helps families of prisoners should avoid financial involvement. Preachers are notoriously soft touches, and seeing great need with little resources to meet it can put them in a position to get "conned" into helping make a rent payment, providing some grocery money until the next check or food stamps come, keeping the utilities from being cut off, and on down an almost endless list of crises calling for money. He should not turn a deaf ear to these needs, and, on occasion, emergency help can be secured from church funds budgeted for the purpose. However, the needs are far more than one minister or even a church can meet, and efforts should be made to meet them by turning to the community agencies previously noted.

Special attention should be given to prisoners' children. They usually have some crucial needs. All too often they are subjected to ridicule and abuse by their peers because of their parent's incarceration, and develop feelings of insecurity and inferiority. They need to feel loved, wanted, and needed, and should be included in Sunday School and missions organizations for their age, especially social activities. Due to the usual poor economic situation in their homes, it is especially important that they be remembered at Christmas with toys, games, and candy or fruit they would not otherwise receive. Prisoners' children exist in a crisis environment. They often develop emotional and behavioral problems. Be ready to recognize this potential difficulty. Help the family to get the services of a professional child guidance clinic, if necessary. If problems at school surface, help by providing volunteer tutors. Of course, the pastor himself cannot do all these things, but he can be aware of the needs and alert responsible people in his church to take steps to help meet them.

Some words of caution need to be repeated: the pastor and volunteers from his church should avoid becoming emotionally involved with convicts' family members, especially children, to the point that they lose a proper sense of perspective. Because of the love of God working in the hearts of those involved in prison ministries, they can become so caught up with people in need that they lose their objectivity. Constant prayer and humility before God are necessary for effective service. If a pastor or worker senses that their involvement with a family is getting out of perspective, steps should be taken to turn them over to another worker or to get the relationship back on an even keel.

In Capsule Form

Inmates are not the only ones affected by their imprisonment. Spouses, children, parents, and friends also feel the impact of his being put away, and offer many opportunities for a pastor and church to help minister to them. Since most jail inmates are men, it is their wives who are put under tremendous stresses in coping with emotional and economic pressures coming as a result of their husbands' incarceration. The pastor and congregation can help by loving concern, visits, helping the family keep in touch, referrals to community service agencies, transportation, and occasional financial assistance. Prisoners' children, especially, stand in need of the loving care and concern of a minister and church workers to help them adjust to abuse, ridicule from peers, and insecurity. God will bless these efforts.

Julio (not his real name) accepted a marked New Testament from the pastor as he visited on the cell block. The next week, he called him into his cell. "I've been reading this book you gave me. I ain't much on reading, but I got a lot outta this. I think what it's talking about is what I really need." He went on to recount a life of crime and deception, which included theft, embezzlement, drug traffic and use, involvement in organized crime, and other infractions of the law. "I've really botched up my life," he said. "D'ya think there's any chance for a guy that's been into as much as I have?" From the Bible, the chaplain showed him verses which pointed out that all manner of sins can be forgiven, and then led him through other verses to a decision for Christ.

The following week, Julio was radiant! He'd gotten a

dictionary to help him, and was devouring the Bible. He was witnessing to others on the cell block. About a month later, he said, "The wife was down here visiting, and she can't understand what's happened to me. I really can't either, but I know that something has, and I really couldn't explain it to her. I want her to know that it's not a 'cop-out'—it's real!"

"Here's my card", the pastor replied; "Next time you talk to her, tell her I'd be glad to come by to see her and explain what's happened to you—but she'll have to invite me."

"Oh, I've told her all about you," Julio said. "I know she'll want to see you. Hey, you mean you really would go over there?"

"If she asks me, I sure will," said the pastor.

A week later she called: "Julio said you'd like to see me."

"Well, he said you were having trouble understanding what has happened to him, and I told him I'd be glad to come tell you," he responded. He went on to explain briefly that what Julio had had was a spiritual experience, and that this was his business—helping others to have this same experience. "And I'd like to just let you read about it out of the Bible." She invited him over for the following Tuesday afternoon.

During the visit the next week, in between the children running in and out, the pastor had the privilege of sharing with Julio's wife what had happened to Julio. He did not press her for a decision at the time, because he could see that all this was completely foreign to her, and he sensed that she was waiting for the "gimmick" or "catch." He asked if she would like for a lady from the church to visit her, and she indicated she would be pleased to have her come by. Julio was really excited about these developments. "Now maybe Maria (not her real name) will understand a little of what I've been trying to tell her!"

The church worker made several visits, heard of Maria's anxieties, frustrations, and apprehensions: "He's so different! But this ain't the first time he's been in there, and he always gets on some kinda of kick when he is. I don't know what to make of it!" After a few visits, the worker invited Maria and the children to Sunday School, and arranged to have them picked up. When a need arose at the church for a paid nursery worker, Maria gladly accepted the opportunity to earn a little extra money.

Christmas drew near, and it became apparent that there was not going to be much for the family. A shopping trip was arranged, and dreams came true for the children Christmas morning. A Christmas basket of groceries and goodies was provided. Maria said, "I know you guys love us. No one has ever done anything like this before."

During another visit in the home, the pastor learned that Maria's father was in the hospital, and went to visit him. Another person heard about Christ's death on the cross for the sins of the whole world, including his. He might never have heard had not a pastor and a church cared. Many who might never be reached otherwise can be won through inmate family ministry.

Notes

1. Duane Pederson, *How to Establish a Jail and Prison Ministry.* (Nashville: Thomas Nelson Publishers, 1979), p. 89.

2. *Mission Action Guide: Prisoner Rehabilitation.* (Memphis: Brotherhood Commission, S.B.C., 1968), p. 14.

3. Pederson, p. 90.

4. Frank Constantino, *Crime Fighter.* (Dallas: Acclaimed Books, 1981), pp. 133-134.

5. Ibid., pp. 102, 104.

6. *Mission Action Guide*, p. 28.
7. *Mission Action Guide*, p. 29.
8. Ibid.
9. *Prison People* (Washington: Prison Fellowship, 1981), p. 48.

7
. . . To All People

"Hey, Rev, when you have a spare minute, I'd like a word with you." Jack is one of the younger corrections officers at the Erie (Pa.) County Prison, where I served as volunteer Protestant chaplain one day a week.

"What about right now?"

"Great!"

He seemed a little nervous. Jack works first shift Sundays at the prison, and thus very seldom gets to the worship services at his church; he didn't even know who the pastor was right then. He talked with me about a disagreement he and his wife were having concerning a child of theirs. Thus the door was opened to share some truths from the Word of God with him.

Jesus said that among "the least of these my brethren" (Matt. 25:36,40) to be ministered to when in need are those in prison. The pastor who goes to jail with the gospel, intent on ministering to those behind bars, often overlooks a whole mission field: the prison staff. They are in prison also; and though, unlike the inmates who are highly restricted, they may come and go as their jobs require, many do not attend church or have any concept of spiritual things.

Who are the officials to whom a chaplain has the opportunity to minister? The most obvious are the institution's staff who have immediate contact with the prisoners: in a jail, the jailers, matrons, bailiffs, and in some cases a teacher, doctor, and social workers; in a prison, the guards, matrons, administrative staff, teachers and instructors, psychologists, doctors and others involved in various aspects of rehabilitation. The chaplain also has opportunities to minister to sheriffs, parole board members, superintendents, marshals, police officers, members of the court from judges down to secretaries, probation officers, wardens, attorneys, and a multitude of other officials within the criminal justice system.

As a chaplain shows genuine interest in these persons and in the work which they do, the Lord will open opportunities to share Christ with them.[1]

When Jesus was born, the angel that appeared to the shepherds said that the "good tidings of great joy" he was bringing to them were to go "to all people".[2] That includes these men and women who have the task of keeping their fellow human beings under lock and key; who serve as their counselors either officially or unofficially; and who administer the system to them in one way or another. Their perceptions of others may be warped by the daily routine of their jobs. The pastor who goes to jail has a unique opportunity to help in their personal and professional lives.

Corrections Officers Are People, Too!

In the course of carrying out his ministry in the jail the preacher may meet counselors, parole and probation officers, deputies, and even attorneys. In the history of prisons, those who held the keys were "guards," and often had little or no training, and more than likely had not done too well at other jobs. Many were merciless with inmates, giving them both verbal and physical abuse. Though there are some vestiges of this, now for the most part prison and jail employees who oversee prisoners are screened in an effort to weed out those with undesirable personality defects and are trained to do their job efficiently and compassionately. The larger the institution, the more likely staff members will have this training. Many have college degrees in criminal justice or a related field; counselors might have a master's degree in social work. Most are married, and have families at home.

Also on the staff are administrative and clerical personnel who may be encountered less frequently, but who also present an opportunity for ministry. Often they are taken for granted; yet their work enables the institution to function smoothly. Some institutions have their own kitchen, which may employ a dietician or other outside help. There are maintenance personnel, too.

So in the jail—but not behind bars—are people from all walks of life. Like those "on the street," they have problems and hopes, needs and victories. One writer says,

> Recognize that the administrative and security personnel at the prison, as well as the inmates, face severe problems and need redemptive change. A prison ministry that is not sensitive to the total needs of the prison is not a complete ministry and will not be helpful to the inmates.[4]

And, ministering to the staff will make it easier to work with the inmates. Ed Stelle, police chaplain for the Portland, Oregon, city-county jails, says,

> You must stay within the framework of the privilege you have been given to work in the jail. Once the jailers understand what you're doing and get to trust you, they'll support you. With prayer, this kind of support can be

established. But once you lose the confidence and trust of the jailers, you can't get it back.[3]

The best way for obtaining the confidence and trust of the staff is by communication and demonstration of interest in them, as well as in the inmates. Duane Pederson says, "The jail staff is often overworked and underpaid, and they may see volunteers as an intrusion and a nuisance. They will need to be convinced that volunteers will help them in some way, or at least not unduly interfere with their responsibilities."[4]

> Ministry to staff . . . is one of the least explored but greatly needed areas of volunteer involvement. Keep in mind that the persons who run the prisons live in the community and need to know Jesus, too. Just think how much more effectively the gospel would be spread if the prison staff were born-again people! I think the importance of this is best pointed out by Chaplain Paul McAfee, Jr., from Albuquerque, New Mexico: "Please emphasize the neglected area of ministry to officers and staff personnel. Volunteers can often have a greater impact on these (especially in outside follow-up) than can the chaplain or other clergy."[5]

The minister who serves the Lord inside the institution should remember that it is his responsibility to take the "good tidings of great joy . . . to *all* people" there: those outside as well as those inside the bars.

All People Have Needs

And those who work inside correctional institutions seem to have as many as others, plus some special job-related ones. The preacher who is alert to these needs will demonstrate that he is knowledgeable, and that he cares.

Those who work most closely with inmates tend to

become calloused, skeptical, and hardened as they come in contact daily with manipulators, con artists, and sociopaths. They witness many inmates turn to "religion" while they are locked up, only to go back to their old ways upon release, and come back to the institution again. Some make sincere efforts to help an inmate, and end up getting "burned" as a result of events either inside the jail or out "on the street" after his release. They receive constant verbal and sometimes physical abuse from prisoners to whom they represent "the system." As they develop contempt for those behind bars, it is returned to them.

Those who work so closely with convicts also tend to become skeptical and critical of volunteers and professional people who try honestly to help; sometimes they will even obstruct their efforts because of the feeling that those who have deliberately broken the law are being "coddled." Many develop animosity and even hatred for inmates and those who seek to minister to them.

For many of the staff, working conditions are less than ideal. Often there is friction between them and the administration, or with supervisors. Shift work places tension on family life, as do the problems that are brought home from work: the resultant domestic stress then aggravates already tight working conditions.

Outside influences also affect the lives of those who serve inside the walls. The courthouse and jail are caught up in the politics of budgeting, and often, the jail comes up short. This has the double result of lower income with higher case load on a less flexible working schedule due to chronic personnel shortages. These factors add to the frustrations of the workers.

Other factors which the pastor who goes to jail will encounter are common to those in his church family: alcohol and drug abuse, marital infidelity, in-law problems,

career clashes, financial stresses—the list could go on and
on. The alert and compassionate man of God will find
plenty of opportunities to help bear the burdens of staff
members and to share with them the unsearchable riches
of Christ from the Word of God.

Ministering to the Needs

How can the preacher develop an extensive ministry to
the jail staff? In this setting, he is a missionary, and can
make practical use of his pastoral training and experience.
The Gospels indicate that Jesus sought to minister to people from all walks of life. Though not "chaplains," Paul
and Silas included the jailer at Philippi in their witness.
And Paul, the missionary prisoner, shared the Word all
the way from Adramyttium to Rome, making sure that his
captors heard about Jesus. An extensive ministry to the
staff may be developed by cultivation, counsel, and conversion.

Cultivation begins with the personal life of the minister.
To be effective for Christ, he must be spiritually prepared,
filled with the Spirit so that he will reflect the Light of the
World. This preparation requires habitual time alone with
God in prayer, and "soaking" in the Word of God, which
means both study and meditation. This personal preparation is essential, not optional. It is only as the pastor who
goes to jail walks with God that he will have the right
motivation for any kind of ministry to prison staff and
inmates.

Cultivation implies an agricultural approach to ministry, and is found throughout the Scriptures. The process
includes preparation of the ground, sowing, weeding, watering, fertilizing, perhaps some plowing between the
rows to loosen the soil, all in expectation of the harvest.
Just to use the word implies passage of time, meaning

simply that a ministry to institutional staff members will not develop overnight.

The preacher should seek to know staff members by name and to learn something about each, without giving the impression of being too inquisitive. It would be helpful to know of birthdays, anniversaries, and other significant events, and to send cards or otherwise express interest. A brief chat in the hall, a cup of coffee together, or fellowship in the lunchroom are among ways to show a personal interest in the individual and to obtain information that will be helpful in ministering to him.

Frequently the minister working behind the bars will come up against security actions such as cell block shakedowns, restricted movement because of a particularly dangerous or notorious inmate, inmate tensions, and the like. These are times when he can, instead of moaning about interruptions or of interference with his ministry, cooperate as part of the team, and at the same time do some of the needed weeding, watering, and fertilizing. As significant changes occur among inmates because of the work of Christ in their hearts, he can share and discuss them with the staff as a part of the sowing process. Pace says, "While some inmates will come to the chaplain or his program completely on their own, for the majority of inmates it is necessary for Christians to take the initiative in establishing the relationship which makes communication possible,"[6] and it is the same with staff members.

I received a telephone call at home from the matron in charge of the women's block at the jail. A new admission was very upset, and was, in turn, disturbing the whole block. She kept insisting that she had to see a "reverend." When she came out of the cell, tears were running down her face, she was sniffling, and was about to tear a handkerchief apart wringing it. In the counseling room she asked, "Is there any way the Lord can forgive me for what I have done?" (She was picked up on a murder charge.)

From the Scriptures, she heard God's promises of forgiveness of "all manner of sin and blasphemy," even though her sins were "as scarlet" and "red like crimson." After prayer, she returned to the matron and to the cell block much more composed.

Half an hour later, when a Bible was brought to the matron to be passed on to the disturbed inmate, the matron asked, "What did you say to her? I've never seen anyone change so much so quickly!" Then the matron listened to the same verses from the Bible that the inmate had heard. The next night, she expressed further amazement at the transformation that had taken place in the previously upset woman, and the door was left open for a continuing witness by the pastor and volunteers from his church who conduct a Bible study on the block.

Counseling may be formal or informal. As the preacher cultivates members of the staff and as they witness changes taking place in some inmates, they may, as did the guard in the earlier incident, ask questions about their own personal problems and needs. Often it will be what Adams calls a "presentation problem"[7] to see how the pastor will handle it. If the response is good, other problems and difficulties may be casually mentioned, and perhaps an appointment set up. It is not within the scope of this presentation to discuss techniques of counseling; rather to point out that if there is to be an effective ministry to the jail staff, the pastor who goes to jail will need to be available for counseling.

This is one reason why his personal preparation is so important. An effective counseling encounter with "Rev" may indeed lead the staff member to suggest to others with whom he is discussing their problems that they look

him up also. A satisfied customer is by far the best adver-
tisement for any product!

Conversion may be one result of counseling, or it may
come as a result of the officer being assigned as security
during the jail chapel service. It is, of course, one of the
reasons for ministry inside the institution. More than likely, it will be a fringe benefit from the preacher's service
in a crisis situation. One writer comments,

> Pastoral care ministry may be understood as growing fun-
> damentally out of the ability to understand what is going
> on in a given human situation with the greatest breadth
> and richness and perception possible, and the accompany-
> ing ability to relate these perceptions to a coherent and
> comprehensive theological framework. Thus ministry in-
> volves a peculiar way of receiving and reflecting on what
> is presented in the human situation at hand.[8]

The wise minister can lead from and through a situation
of tenseness and confusion to the peace that passes all
understanding in Christ Jesus. And, again, though the
new believer at first may say nothing to his peers about
his experience, the changes in his life will not be lost on
them, either.

Conservation has to do with keeping that which is
gained. Changes inside a jail are hard to come by and take
place very slowly as they seep down through various ech-
elons of administration and authority. Constant effort is
required not only to make progress, but also not to lose
the ground that has been gained. Writing in the *AEIC
Journal,* Gerald R. Chancellor observes:

> In too many religious circles, correctional ministries in-
> cluded, there is a common practice with reference to new
> converts called "dippin' em and droppin' 'em." This is a
> highly rationalized practice of evangelism that is so inter-

ested in the numbers of "souls being saved" that little or no attention is given to spiritual nurture toward Christian maturity. The wide-spread practice has produced a whole host of "alka-seltzer" Christians who have hardly hit the water (baptism) before they have fizzled out. This spiritual tragedy and travesty of the divine gospel has not entirely escaped the ranks of correctional chaplains, either.[9]

As with inmates, the minister should encourage staff members to have a personal devotional life of Bible study and prayer. He is in a unique position to point out the practical uses of the Word of God. Christian psychologist Wayne Oates writes,

> The pastor who uses the Bible as a means of interpretation, comfort, and prayer in his individual pastoral ministry cannot be dominated by the concepts of men and women who are functioning in a secular environment, and who do not accept any responsibility for the religious life of the persons with whom they work.[10]

This is true also of staff members, both new and mature believers, who probably have more contact with the preacher who goes to jail than they do with their own pastors. They can be provided with literature designed to strengthen them in the faith or lead them to Christ as their case may be. There could be the offer of a brief mealtime Bible study or devotional time just for them. And, of course, they should be encouraged not only to attend, but also to participate actively in a Bible-preaching church with their families. The minister can allot a certain portion of his schedule for the staff, and let it be known that he is available then to assist them in any way he can.

In Spirit-led cultivation, an extensive ministry to the staff of a correctional institution can be developed.

In a Few Short Words

"But when he saw the multitudes, he was moved with compassion on them, because they fainted, and were scattered abroad, as sheep having no shepherd" (Matt. 9:36).

Inside the jails and prisons are not only hundreds of thousands of offenders who need ministry, but also tens of thousands of men and women who, though they may leave the institution once their hours are completed, are nevertheless affected by their contacts with inmates and their families. In addition to the usual human and spiritual needs of others, they have special ones related to their jobs or professions. Some, having no spiritual frame of reference, are just giving up, and going on down the broad way that leads to destruction. Others who know the Lord have their paths fogged by attitudes of inmates, peers, and administration, and are bitter, angry, and confused, The pastor who goes to jail has the opportunity to serve the Lord in ministering to these public servants. They should not be overlooked in the rush to get the gospel message to the inmates.

In my pocket as I walked up to the guard station before going onto the cell block was a tract, "What Must I Do to Be Saved?"

"Hey, lemme see that," said the officer, pointing to it. Looking for awhile at the title, he said, "That's what I need, to be saved!"

"You mean you've gotten this far, and it hasn't happened to you yet?"

"Well, I go to church just about every Sunday, say my prayers, and read the Bible some, but, well, I can't really explain it—something's missing!"

"If you want to, I can let you read right out of here (Bible appears) what it is you're looking for."

"I ain't got nuttin' special to do 'til we lock up for chow." Right there at the guard station, with another officer looking on, this man read from the Scriptures what he needed to know, and in prayer asked Jesus to come into his heart!

At a banquet for chaplains and would-be chaplains, the speaker, a sheriff at a county jail, said, "If you don't remember anything else I'm saying tonight, I hope you will remember this: Your job is to minister *to all people.*"

Notes

1. Dale K. Pace, *A Christian's Guide to Effective Jail and Prison Ministries.* (Old Tappan, N.J.: Fleming H. Revell Co., 1976), pp. 157-158.

2. Paul D. Schoonmaker, *The Prison Connection.* (Valley Forge, Pa.,: Judson Press, 1978), p. 76.

3. Duane Pederson, *How to Establish a Jail and Prison Ministry.* (Nashville: Thomas Nelson Publishers, 1979), p. 52.

4. Ibid.

5. Frank Constantino, *Crime Fighter.* (Dallas: Acclaimed Books, 1981), p. 52.

6. Pace, page 167.

7. Jay E. Adams, *Competent to Counsel* (Grand Rapids, Mich.,: Baker Book House, 1970), p. 148.

8. Charles V. Gerkin, *Crisis Experience in Modern Life.* (Nashville: Abingdon Press, 1979), p. 12.

9. Gerald R. Chancellor, "Follow-Up Inside the Institution," *AEIC Journal,* July, 1981, p. 10.

10. Wayne E. Oates, *The Bible and Pastoral Care.* (Grand Rapids, Mich.,: Baker Book House, 1971), p. 12.

8
A Final Word

There is a lot of talk these days about jail and prison ministry, but not enough is being done. It is difficult and frustrating, but it does offer the possibility of great rewards.

> I don't want to give you the idea that building a relationship with an inmate is a smooth process from initial introduction to coming to a knowledge of Christ. This is not the case with persons outside prisons, and it is certainly not true for those in prisons. . . .
>
> It may help to recall Jesus' parable of the sower of the seed and the four kinds of soil upon which the seed fell. Inmates, like everyone else, will fit into one of these four types of responsiveness to the gospel. As a volunteer, you must be sensitive to this problem of false profession without becoming cynical about every profession of faith. . . . You will need prayer, faithfulness, and spiritual discernment for this work—a high standard, but our service for Jesus demands nothing less.[1]

In another parable, Jesus taught His followers that they should go out into the streets and lanes of the city and into the highways and hedges of the countryside in order that those who need to hear of His invitation of salvation by grace through faith might have the opportunity (Luke 14:15-24). Usually right on one of those streets, mostly in

the center of the city, is a building which houses sometimes just a few, sometimes hundreds, many of whom are
defeated, discouraged, and depressed; obstinate and rebellious; violent and profane; and some are humbled and
repentant, open to receive His invitation. Their decisions
for Christ and their spiritual growth under less-than-ideal
circumstances can be a source of rejoicing and praise for
the pastor who goes to jail.

Note

1. Duane Pederson, *How to Establish a Jail and Prison Ministry.* (Nashville:
Thomas Nelson Publishers, 1979), pp. 71-72.

Appendix:
Excerpts from Unsolicited
Inmate Letters

Am writing to you concerning a matter that has become very important to me. As you know from our previous conversations, I've had the feeling that God has been knocking upon the door of my heart. Well, a few days ago, I opened that door for Him to enter and committed myself to Him. I signed that check you gave me on the Eternal Bank of Christ and I am going to do everything in my power to keep it from bouncing. I want God in my heart and in my life. I want the remaining part of my life here on earth dedicated to Him and His wishes.

I really felt something last night by letting God into my heart. It's like a lot of weight being lifted off my shoulders. I was glad that we had our little talk. I've really sinned for the past ten years. Went to bed with men and women and stealing and telling lies. And now I am glad that I was saved, and my cell mate is glad I was saved, too. Some people don't care if they are saved or not. But I do! Because I want to be like the Lord Jesus Christ when He comes back to this world.

Rev, I just want to thank you for showing me the way to the Lord Jesus and if it were not for you takeing the time I would have never found the happiness that I have with the Lord Jesus. . . . I am so happy to have a friend like the Lord Jesus because He is the one friend that will not let me down.

I just thought I would write you a letter and let you no I am fine and that God is still with me and when I came down here I thought I would not like it out there a lot of Brother in the Lord down here and all we do is talk about the Lord Jesus and get other ones to here about our Lord and it is really nice to tell someone else about Jesus and how he has come into our life and took us from sin.

In Pittsburgh, at the County Prison, I ran across one of the guards who knew me "way back when," and after we talked for about an hour or so, he said, "Man . . . what's happened to you? You ain't the same guy!" I'm not! I'm somebody completely different, in all ways, even though at some times the old self tryes to jump out, it's suppressed by the Spirit. Why? Because I asked Him to!

I really appreciate that you listen to my problem and pray with me every time you came to teach the Bible. And your teaching brought good feeling to my soul. I thank you very much.

. . . so I also would like to get my G.E.D. diploma and make something useful out of my life. And I would like to become or take up being a minister so I can help others find the Lord just as I have done with your help. And I thank you for all the help you have given me mentally and spiritually because I have come to know the Lord more each day and if it wasn't for you, I may never have found Him.

I just wish I had known Jesus as my Saviour long before this, but who knows I may have never excepted Jesus if I was out on the streets. But what really counts is that I have him (God) now and I never want to leave him. Because I know he will never leave me so I have nothing to worry about.

I had to write you and tell you that I was very happy to hear from you and your church. The Lord must truely have his hand in this situation. I pray that he guides you into teaching me about our most precious Jesus. It is really hard to live the Christian life here in jail. I am so glad you try and help us who are lost.

I remember when you first came you were leary of the people but as time passed by there were a lot of people whom were happy to see you each week. You brought a lot of inspiration to many people, myself included. I really hope that you have continued to work with people in prison. There are so many people in prison that don't have family or friends for moral support, and without people such as yourself.

Did you get to talk to my Mom? I have been writing to her and trying to explain to her how she can except Jesus as her Saviour, but I don't know if she understands but I'll keep trying. I hope you would go and see her, because I feel she wants to except but she isn't sure. I have to start writing to my sister to see if she will except Christ. It will be hard because we haven't written or seen each other since my dad's death.

I am down here and doing good because I know that

God is in here with me and he is helping me to understand myself better than I ever did before. I know I have made mistakes and that he's forgave me for them. Now I am praying that my family someday forgives me to and I know with God's help it will happen.

Bibliography

AEIC Journal. Richmond, Va.: Association of Evangelical Institutional Chaplains, published semiannually.

Brown, Jack, *Monkey Off My Back.* Grand Rapids, Mich.,: Zondervan Publishing House, 1971.

Collins, Gary, *How to Be a People Helper.* Santa Ana, Calif.: Vision House Publishers, 1976.

Colson, Charles W., *Born Again.* Old Tappan, N.J.: Fleming H. Revell Co., 1976.

————, *Life Sentence.* Lincoln, Va.: Chosen Books, 1979.

Constantino, Frank, *Crime Fighter.* Dallas: Acclaimed Books, 1981.

Ellul, Jacques, *Violence.* New York: The Seabury Press, 1969.

Fox, Vernon, *Introduction to Corrections.* Englewood Cliffs, N.J.: Fleming H. Revell Co., 1972.

Gerkin, Charles V., *Crisis Experience in Modern Life.* Nashville: Abingdon Press, 1979.

Glass, Bill, *Free At Last.* Waco, Texas: Word Books, 1971.

Graham, Jerry, *Where Flies Don't Land.* Plainfield, N.J.: Logos International, 1977.

Hoekstra, Ray, *God's Prison Gang.* Old Tappan, N.J.: Fleming H. Revell Co., 1977.

Holy Bible, King James Version, Thompson Chain Refer-

ence Edition. Indianapolis: B.B. Kirkbride Bible Co., 1964.

Jefferson, Ted, *One Bad Dude.* Grand Rapids: Baker Book House, 1978.

Mission Action Guide: Prisoner Rehabilitation. Memphis: Brotherhood Commission, S.B.C., 1968.

Oates, Wayne E., *The Bible and Pastoral Care.* Grand Rapids: Baker Book House, 1971.

One-on-One Discipleship Handbook. Arlington, Va.: Good New Mission, 1978.

Pace, Dale K., *A Christian's Guide to Effective Jail and Prison Ministries.* Old Tappan, N.J.: Fleming H. Revell Co., 1976.

Pederson, Duane, *How To Establish a Jail and Prison Ministry.* Nashville: Thomas Nelson Publishers, 1979.

Prison People. Arlington, Va.: Prison Fellowship, 1981.

Rutledge, Howard and Phyllis, *In the Presence of Mine Enemies.* Old Tappan, N.J.: Fleming H. Revell Co., 1973.

Schoonmaker, Paul D., *The Prison Connection.* Valley Forge, Pa.: Judson Press, 1978.

ten Boom, Corrie, *He Sets the Captive Free.* Old Tappan, N.J.: Fleming H. Revell Co., 1977.

Thomas, Cal, *A Freedom Dream.* Waco: Word Books, 1977.

Vaus, Jim, *The Devil Loves a Shining Mark.* Waco: Word Books, 1974.

Volunteer Worker Handbook. Arlington, Va.: Good News Mission, n.d.

Watson, Tex, *Will You Die for Me?* Old Tappan, N.J.: Fleming H. Revell Co., 1978.